PENGUIN CANADA

THE WEEKENDER

ROY MacGREGOR has been a journalist
for more than thirty years, and for the
past decade, a regular contributor to
Cottage Life magazine with his immensely
popular "Weekender" column. He is the
author of numerous bestselling and
award-winning books, including *Escape*,
Canoe Lake, *A Life in the Bush*, *The Home Team*,
and the popular children's mystery series
The Screech Owls. His next essay collection,
The Dog and I, will be published in 2006.
MacGregor was named an officer in the
Order of Canada in 2005 and currently
resides in Kanata, Ontario.

D0887820

ALSO BY ROY MacGREGOR

Escape: In Search of the Natural Soul of Canada

A Loonie for Luck

A Life in the Bush

Canoe Lake

The Home Team

Road Games

Chief: The Fearless Vision of Billy Diamond

Home Game *(with Ken Dryden)*

The Screech Owl Mystery Series *(for young readers)*

THE

Weekender

A COTTAGE JOURNAL

Roy MacGregor

PENGUIN
CANADA

PENGUIN CANADA

Published by the Penguin Group

Penguin Group (Canada), 90 Eglinton Avenue East, Suite 700, Toronto, Ontario, Canada M4P 2Y3
    (a division of Pearson Canada Inc.)

Penguin Group (USA) Inc., 375 Hudson Street, New York, New York 10014, U.S.A.
Penguin Books Ltd, 80 Strand, London WC2R 0RL, England
Penguin Ireland, 25 St Stephen's Green, Dublin 2, Ireland (a division of Penguin Books Ltd)
Penguin Group (Australia), 250 Camberwell Road, Camberwell, Victoria 3124, Australia
    (a division of Pearson Australia Group Pty Ltd)
Penguin Books India Pvt Ltd, 11 Community Centre, Panchsheel Park, New Delhi – 110 017, India
Penguin Group (NZ), cnr Airborne and Rosedale Roads, Albany, Auckland 1310, New Zealand
    (a division of Pearson New Zealand Ltd)
Penguin Books (South Africa) (Pty) Ltd, 24 Sturdee Avenue, Rosebank, Johannesburg 2196, South Africa

Penguin Books Ltd, Registered Offices: 80 Strand, London WC2R 0RL, England

First published in a Viking Canada hardcover by Penguin Group (Canada),
    a division of Pearson Canada Inc., 2005
Published in this edition, 2006

(RRD) 10 9 8 7 6 5 4 3 2 1

Text copyright © Roy MacGregor, 2005
Illustrations copyright © Jason Schneider, 2005

All rights reserved. Without limiting the rights under copyright reserved above, no part of this
publication may be reproduced, stored in or introduced into a retrieval system, or transmitted in
any form or by any means (electronic, mechanical, photocopying, recording or otherwise), without
the prior written permission of both the copyright owner and the above publisher of this book.

Manufactured in the U.S.A.

ISBN-10: 0-14-305260-8
ISBN-13: 978-0-14-305260-9

Library and Archives Canada Cataloguing in Publication data available upon request.

Except in the United States of America, this book is sold subject to the condition that it shall not, by
way of trade or otherwise, be lent, re-sold, hired out, or otherwise circulated without the publisher's
prior consent in any form of binding or cover other than that in which it is published and without a
similar condition including this condition being imposed on the subsequent purchaser.

Visit the Penguin Group (Canada) website at **www.penguin.ca**

Special and corporate bulk purchase rates available; please see
www.penguin.ca/corporatesales or call 1-800-399-6858, ext. 477 or 474

For Lloyd and Rose Griffith,
with appreciation

Contents

Introduction x

April 23—First breath of spring I

Opening Up 3

Cottage Mice 9

April 30—Eccentricities 13

The Cottage Handyman 14

May 21—Ritual 18

The First Long Weekend 19

The First Swim 22

The First Paddle 25

May 30—Bugged 29

Mosquitoes 30

June 12—In awe 34

The Power of Nature 35

June 18—Dock talk 38

The Ministry Moose 39

Crokinole 43

June 25—Heading out 47

The Lure of Summer 49

The "Stupid Stop" 55

June 27—The Great Canadian Debate 59

July versus August 60

July 1—Settling in 64

Canada Day 65

Cottage Reading 69

July 10—Summer rhythms 74

The Cottage Dump 75

Fishing 79

Town Survival Manual 85

July 13—Curiosities 88

The Snapping Turtle 89

The Art of Puttering 93

The Fish Finder 98

July 23—Passages 102

Kicked Out 103

July 25—Feelings 115

The Head Injury 116

Sounds 119

Gold Fever 127

August 6—Local chatter 130

Bears at the Dump 131

Locals versus Tourists 135

August 8—Deeply personal 139

Digging out the Outhouse 140

The Annual Canoe Trip 143

August 28—Turning over 149

The Cat Who Went Missing 150

Labour Day Weekend 155

September 10—Stung 160

The Official Canadian Bug Off 161

Car Hits Bear 164

September 18—Spaces 167

Maps 168

Dog Years and Human Years 172

September 26—Taking measure 176

The Woodpile 177

"Progress" Comes to the Lake 181

The Flying Squirrel 188

October 11—Closing up 191

Thanksgiving Unplugged 192

November 26—In awe 200

The Northern Lights 201

December 26—Christmas break 205

Ice 207

January 1—Extreme cottaging 212

Winter Cottaging 213

Subnivian 218

March 19—Winter break 222

March Break 223

The World's Largest Rink 226

March 29—Full circle 229

The Cottage of the Mind 230

Warm Spots 233

April 16—Promise 237

Acknowledgments 238

Introduction

On the cork wall in my little office, where everything from dental appointments to unpaid bills is tacked up so they won't be forgotten, there are two different sets of directions for getting to our cabin at the lake. They are stored there for handing out to friends, usually friends of the children; we, of course, could no more forget the way than a Pacific salmon would not know which river to head up. One version contains printed directions (*"turn left at the third exit for Renfrew"*) and the other is a crudely drawn map, by my own hand, showing a long and wiggly line that goes beyond Renfrew all the way to the western edge of Algonquin Park, where a big "X" marks the spot as if hidden treasure were to be found there.

Which, of course, it is.

What was it Ishmael said of Queequeg's distant island home in *Moby Dick*? "It's not down on any map; true places never are." Well, *this* true place is—even if the map is in worse proportion than Popeye's arms.

The map on the corkboard shows a badly connected circle called Eganville, but says nothing about the Ottawa Valley chip wagon up hard against the town liquor store, two important stops on any journey to the cabin. The printed version says "Go through Barry's Bay" but says nothing about Grumblin' Granny's eclectic store and the routine stops while the three daughters sift through cotton dresses from South America and our son heads down the street to check out the latest fishing lures.

From Ottawa, it takes four hours to get to that "X" if you're in a hurry, five if you include those stops and at least one more through the Park. Technically, you are supposed to pay a $12 visitor's fee for making any use of Park facilities, but we presume that involves swimming and hiking, not pee breaks, which we consider a necessity, if not a rite of passage.

We take a route so familiar that the car almost drives itself: north on the 417 until it reduces to the two-lane Highway 17 heading north and west along the Ottawa River to Renfrew, then west on Highway 60 into the huge park where my mother was born, my father worked, and our grandparents once lived year-round in a magnificent log house on a dramatic rocky point on the north shore of Lake of Two Rivers.

Ghosts live there now and I always wave, but sometimes in fine weather—still a good hour from our destination—

we will stop and dive off the high rocks and turn the five-hour trip into six.

I was only three days old when my parents brought me here to the old log home my ranger grandfather built, the first "cottage" I ever knew. The cottage was sold to an American couple in the 1960s, following the death of our grandparents, and, in the 1970s, the new owners had the logs dismantled and carted away to be reassembled on the grounds of a Muskoka lodge. I have never been to see what it looks like because, of course, it could not possibly look right. There is nothing standing on the rocky point today but the trees, and only a hint of the spectacular granite and quartz fireplace the old ranger put in with his own hands. But readers will understand when I say it still burns.

The two sleeping cabins and the summer kitchen at the end of the point have vanished, as has the dock that was large enough to tie down a Lands and Forests floatplane in a high wind, but the roots and rocks feel to my middle-aged bare feet much as they did a half-century back when older brother Jim and sister Ann would lead younger brother Tom and I along them in a game of imaginary life and death.

Once we have had our stop at Lake of Two Rivers, we travel on past Cache Lake, Source Lake, Canoe Lake, Smoke Lake, Tea Lake, and the Oxtongue River—names that are, to me, like the first notes of a favourite song. From the Oxtongue we pass quickly through the tiny village of Dwight and on toward Huntsville, turning north about halfway between Dwight and Huntsville on a road so beautifully named, *Limberlost,* that it describes itself.

Twenty minutes later, having passed a deeply religious community, Mizpah, that is today nothing but a fascinating pioneer cemetery on the edge of the dump, we slip by a summer camp, where the bush then squeezes in and the paved hardtop eventually peters out into gravel. We turn off the gravel road to little more than a path, and, down a long dip toward the lake, we are suddenly at a place even better than "home."

It is nothing but a simple, rustic building—plank siding stained brown and grey, a green roof, rectangular, with a long deck on the lakeside, an outhouse up the hill to the west, and a shed where the cars are parked. A burglar would be disappointed. There is nothing worth taking. The treasures we carry with us in our heads.

Some of these treasures I have tried to record—most faithfully, a few with wild exaggeration—over the years on the back page of a remarkable magazine called *Cottage Life.* The "Weekender" column has been a gift to me from publisher Al Zikovitz, my old hockey winger, and his superb editors, Ann Vanderhoof, then David Zimmer, now Penny Caldwell and Catherine Collins.

They have no idea the privilege they afford me—the chance to write about the place I love most in all this world. This book comes in part out of those columns and features for this enchanting publication, and also from those columns I have done on life at the lake for the *Ottawa Citizen*, the *National Post*, and *The Globe and Mail*. Many of the columns and features have been reworked and recast for reasons of continuity and time; many appear exactly as they were first written. Interspersed throughout are small journal entries abridged from and modelled after the cottage journal I have kept for more than twenty years. We are now well into our third volume and it has become, somehow, such a daily ritual that God be with the family member or visitor who does not sit down and record something significant about the day just past. A blank page is, in this ritual-bound world at the edge of the lake, a crime roughly as serious as failing to take a replacement roll of toilet paper up the hill.

I began keeping a journal, somewhat awkwardly, on Saturday, July 23, 1983. The cottage—it belonged to Ellen's parents—had never had a journal, and the previous fifteen years of the little cabin's existence had been recorded on a haphazard series of tree fungi and a stack of old calendars noting how many fish had been caught and how much the official recording secretary claimed they had weighed.

My grandfather, on the other hand, had always kept a daily journal. The old ranger would take a sharpened pencil, open the little tally book, and record the weather—wind, temperature, sun, rain or snow—and where he had gone that day. Nothing else: no personal observations, no anecdotes. Just the bare facts of a job. His influence must have been felt that first entry I made in our first journal, for it reads as spare and straightforward as if he had pencilled it in himself: *"Arrived around suppertime. Weather fine."* The evolution began the very next day—*"Clouded over, slight drizzle"*—but now with a note that cousin Tom Pigeou was out to help bring down a difficult hemlock, a reference to the youngest daughter's very first fish (a perch), and a mention that the grandmothers had come out from town for supper.

It is fascinating, with more than two decades' perspective, to sit here and see how the cottage journal changed. Gradually, the entries grew longer. The weather became incidental, and the real meat of the exercise soon became the stories and tales of what happened. Less about the lack of sun and much more about the abundance of turtles, the joy of a long rope hanging from a tree branch, the success (or failure) of a certain trick over the wake, the old and new friends dropping by, the progress of the lake's baby loons ...

There is something to be said for photographs, but something, as well, to be said *against* them. There is also something not entirely accurate about the summers they record. Everyone seems always to be tied to each other by ropes and they are always smiling and the sun is always shining and they are usually taken, unfortunately, after an event of such enormous impact that someone has finally thought to run for the camera.

A journal is different. It tells us what it was like the day the rain seemed to be ringing off the lake. It captures the sense of defeat the losers must surely feel—for how would *I* know?—at the end of a Monopoly or Risk game that goes on past midnight. It also reminds us of times that are significant only in the small history of a family: first swim, even, sad to say, *last* fish.

Ours is a book by many authors, with children and visitors invited to write whatever they felt about whatever happened that particular day at the cottage. Some of the children's entries come complete with illustrations, and they are prized as much as if they were sketched by the Group of Seven. Some of the entries are by those who are no longer here but whose presence is felt, and will always be felt, in every corner of this little property on the side of the lake.

It is the record of our times, and the one part of cottage life that opens up and closes up dozens of times a year. No tools required.

"I do not understand," Marjorie Kinnan Rawlings wrote in her 1942 masterpiece on nature, *Cross Creek,* "how anyone can live without some small place of enchantment to turn to."

It doesn't really matter whether we call it cottage or camp, whether it is owned or rented or borrowed, whether it is one of the $9.5-million monstrosities of the Muskoka lakes, a simple, banged-up camper trailer on the banks of a northern river, or a park campsite you need to book months in advance: they are all equal in the state of mind they produce. For those of us fortunate enough to have access to such a place, whether by ownership, by invitation, or by booking ahead, it is where we *summer* and, virtually by definition, the place we treasure most.

The reason for this odd state of mind—or, more accurately, state of *values*—is absurdly clear to those Canadians who have waited through bleak, wet, and windy falls; long and difficult winters; and springs that start and finish in a single May afternoon. Summer is our secret time, the few precious weeks when we believe we are our truest selves. No matter how it exists in reality, the summer place remains, for so many of us, our sweetest thought, one held in parentheses by the opening up and the closing up of the cottage, quite often the happiest and saddest days of a given year.

The cottage—or the cabin, or the camp, if you prefer—is an idea that rubs against the soul of Canadians like a friendly cat that greets you at the front door after a lousy day of work. It is, both in imagination and reality, who we are, our statement on the bush and the north and the seasons.

It is the way we homestead on summer, as if it might be somehow possible to build a better life away from the April muck and November sleet and January hopelessness. It is the way Canadians shake off our cluttered city lives and are permitted to pioneer momentarily away from the madness and stress.

It is where we would live, if only we could figure out how.

April 23

S	M	T	W	T	F	S
				1	2	3
4	5	6	7	8	9	10
11	12	13	14	15	16	17
18	19	20	21	22	(23)	24
25	26	27	28	29	30	

11°C. Cool and windy. But the sun is out and feels wonderful on the face and bare arms. It's a peculiarity of the Canadian psyche that, if you had this exact same day in early November, you'd be wrapped in fleece jackets and windbreakers. Everyone is outside—everyone, including the dog, just a little bit crazy as if school had let out for the summer, even though summer doesn't officially begin for another two months. Even when we may have come a couple of times over the winter, spring is still the "first" trip of the year. The winter trips are to see how you survive, the spring trip to see how the cottage survived.

Opening Up

Now is when we begin the most important journey of the year. It will have been planned and talked about for weeks, and yet there will still be a last-minute scramble to get going. We will take the same route that this particular family has taken now for more than a quarter of a century— and yet we will still notice flowering dogwood and pin cherry as if never before having seen such marvels.

We will wonder, again, why such fuss is made of fall colours—the red and rust of maple—while nothing is said of the stunning varieties of purple in a hardwood forest about to leaf. Is it simply because spring arrives without melancholy in Canada? Is bittersweet sadness such a part of the fall equation in this country that we feel compelled to stare in amazement and record in pictures, as if preserving, the one season—while we seem perfectly willing to skip this other right into summer? Or is it simply because the Canadian calendar divides no more easily into quarters than Gaul did for Caesar? Summer we would extend forever; winter already seems to stretch forever; fall, *nice* fall, is fleeting; but spring— spring lasts about a full afternoon in a good year, just enough time for the runoff to take place and the big coats to come off.

I have grown to treasure that first spring trip in from the main highway. I will roll the window down, even if the air is still cool, and let the smells of spring race about our heads as we scream and sing our way closer and closer to whatever surprises await us.

Sometimes, if we arrive late, there will be fox kittens warming themselves on the north side of the final hill on the approach to the lake. Sometimes there will be moose tracks on the soft sand where we turn in. Always, the lake will be high from the spring runoff in Algonquin Park and the docks will be floating well above the rocks we have piled for support. One year these docks had broken free from their safety ties and were blown far down the lake, where they rested, safely, in a sheltered bay until we towed them back and re-fastened them to the shore.

The ancient aluminum cartopper will be tipped from the cedar it was leaned against the previous fall and the forty-year-old Johnson 6 hp and its scratched and dented gas tank hauled from the shed. One of us will yank the starter rope a dozen times or more, jam the throttle in and out, and perhaps even curse a few times before a blue flume of smoke rises and the engine roars into action. Usually there will be floating logs that have been set free by the shifting ice and we will need to lasso them and tow them to a far bay—the bone yard—where they will hopefully stay fast until the next breakup.

The work at first seems endless: branches and leaves to clear, chimneys and eavestrough to check, a deck to sweep, and old chairs to set out. The docks must be tightened and supported by rocks at the shallow end and metal pipes at the deep. The canoe will be taken down and gently dropped off the end of a dock for a quick spin of the bay just to make sure the "J" stroke didn't get forgotten over the winter. The barbecue must be carried down from the outhouse, cleaned, and fired up. There are inner tubes to blow up, pails to clean, a refrigerator to plug in, floors to sweep, and—in the sweetest ceremony of all—the first cold beer to be had on the deck, no matter the weather.

At some point, after we've cranked up the fireplace, I will reach up onto the top of the refrigerator, take down the journal, and make note of what is, really, the joyous beginning of the year for us. It strikes me, however, that a distant archaeologist coming across these various notebooks might not quite understand what exactly we are celebrating:

May 20, 1984: Blackflies unbearable!—chimney replaced, cooked a goose and it fell on the floor, two-year-old Gordon burned hand on fire box …

May 16, 1987: Ten of us spread through three bedrooms—A bit chaotic and cool … power went out around 9:30. No candles.

May 21, 1988: Bugs—blackflies—worst in memory.

May 20, 1989: Rainy and cool—could see breath out on water!—but no one cares. We're at the cottage, and everything is new again.

Everything is new again. New in the late 1960s, when this place was built by those who are no longer here; new in the late 1970s, when the first of the grandchildren arrived; new in the 1980s, when we began taking over; new in the 1990s; new still in the 21st century. Reborn every spring— no matter how bad the bugs. It is our annual "coming out." And the happiest moment of our fleeting spring— even if there is still a thin pane of ice forming around the shore each morning—comes when the cabin is officially opened for the year.

Perhaps I have inherited this sense of "coming to life again" from my grandparents, who spent their retirement wintering in various villages and towns around the province, counting the days until they could head back to Algonquin Park and Lake of Two Rivers and the lives they found far more rewarding than a few rented rooms and central heating. Once the sun had melted enough snow for them to pull safely off the main road, they were ready to head in for "The Season," and, even with old age stalking them, they would not be held back by any protest from their five children.

Today, this little cabin has increasingly become the same place to our four children as the grandparents' log home on Lake of Two Rivers once was to a previous generation. The roles have changed, and, if there is one wish worth having, it is that one day we become the elderly grandparents refusing to give in and give up.

At some point, perhaps between the second and third beer, talk will turn, as it always does, to projects, for the Canadian summer is, in so many ways, a neverending series of best-laid plans. *This will be the summer that I put a cover over the woodpile ... This will be the summer that we paint the deck ... This will be the summer when we finally haul that old stove oil drum off to the dump ... This will be the summer when we finally put in water ...*

Some of them, obviously, do get done. But it hardly matters. Soon, far too soon, this marvellous season that begins in sparklers will end in embers. Almost precisely the same weather that so promises in May will mysteriously threaten in October, almost as if life had somehow reversed itself. Relief will then be found inside rather than out. What months ago was the exceptional pleasure of Opening Up will become the onerous task of Closing Up— with the sole comfort coming from the fact that, in half a year or so it will again be time to Open Up.

It is, simply, the life cycle of the Canadian cottager—not so different, appropriately, from the loons that arrive as soon as the ice goes out and leave, mournfully calling out to the rest of the world, just before freeze-up.

This, however, is Opening Up, and Closing Up seems so far off it does not even warrant consideration. Opening Up is when The Season begins—the only one of the four that needs no qualifier. And the only one of the four we try and spread as far as possible into the spring and fall that bracket it.

Cottage Mice

They are the original time sharers. They take the bulk of the year, often the best days. They have the run of the place. They stay up all night, eat our food, refuse to clean up after themselves, and don't pay a cent toward the taxes. They are cottage mice—and right now, for those human summer dwellers who are not at their sacred retreats know, they are urinating and defecating over the very things you love most in the world.

It is more than 2500 years since Aesop tried to explain the differences between the Town Mouse and the Country Mouse—both charming domestic pets compared with the Cottage Mouse—and we have to believe if he were writing today in, say, Bobcaygeon, Ontario, instead of Samos, Greece, he would pass on the fable and go directly to the murder-mystery. The real puzzle to solve would be the choice of weapon.

I speak as someone who, for decades, blissfully forgot about mice. We had none. They were other cottagers' headaches. Come spring I might find a small nest of leaves and boat cushion stuffing in an old swim mask stored in the shed down by the water—once in a while complete with tiny pink newborns—but never, ever in the old hermetically sealed cabin up the hill, where not a single hole had been drilled in the floor or wall since it was built. All that changed the moment we decided to modernize. For more money than it costs to put a child through university, we got a septic system that would pass inspection in the Municipality of Heaven, a flush toilet, running water … and mice.

I once argued that the most distinctive sound of summer is the slam of a screen door. It now seems I had forgotten the night sounds from my youth in Algonquin Park, the sudden *snap* of a trap going off, the tiny thrashing that, on a still July evening in the imagination of a child, becomes the equivalent of a World Wrestling Entertainment "smackdown" until, eventually, the trap-flipping, scuffling, and dragging peter out and the sleepless can lie there awaiting the next execution.

For twenty years and more there had been no such sound in this particular cottage. The travails of other cottagers were simple amusement for us. One woman on the lake said it sounded in her ancient log cabin as if the mice were constructing "elevator shafts" in the walls at night. One man, blessed—or perhaps in this case cursed—with three lovely and sensitive young children, spent the equivalent of a Disney World trip on various live traps, his boat operating as an early morning limousine service for the unimpressed mice as he ferried them over to "Mouse Island," released them, and motored back—I'm sure barely beating the tiny swimmers back to his dock.

Now, however, *we* had mice, and suddenly it was not so funny. We set cheap Victor traps with cheese, woke at night to the sounds of carnage, and in the morning hauled the dead out to the bush. The traps worked fine until a daughter arrived with her new Boston Terrier—a dog of no known purpose, approximately the size of a mouse on steroids, roughly similar in appearance to a wingless bat— and the *snap* of a back bedroom trap was instantly followed by the howls of a puppy that should be grateful it was bred, for no apparent reason, to have no discernible snout.

We switched to Warfarin, poison, but there being no evidence it was working—supposedly the mice feed and then wander off somewhere to die like old elephants—we decided to abandon all form of trap and poison and, instead, take the battle outside. Every possible hole in the building was then filled with steel wool packed so tightly not even a Cabinet document could leak through it.

The puppy and its swollen nose having returned to the city, we set out Victor traps again, caught three more mice, and then, magically, there were no more. But still I worry. I worry that there is not one but two still there, and that they are male and female. I worry, because I have read that a single pair of cottage mice could produce 2500 offspring in a single year, that a single pair alone would leave behind 46,000 droppings on the kitchen counter and dining table and 1.4 litres of mouse urine on the bed clothes, the carpet, and, for all I know, in the sacred baseball cap that must be worn while trout fishing.

If mice are, in fact, still getting in, I will move immediately to sign a formal time-share agreement: Leave it exactly as you found it. And that includes Victor traps, fully baited and set.

April 30

14°C. Partly cloudy. Fraser has the shed done! It is, as everything he builds, a work of perfection, an edifice that took much longer to build than was ever expected. But this is how he works and no one would ever want it, or expect it, differently. We almost hesitate to defile his creation by filling it with tools. Fraser is family now. He grew up in town, went to school with my brother Tom, studied engineering, but then one day decided he wanted to be his own boss and went into carpentry—though he also does electrical work, plumbing, and psychological counselling. When the dog got so old she had to be carried up the steps, he built her a "wheelchair ramp" and refused to charge for either the materials or his labour. He has his own chair on the deck, and to watch him with a coffee and a smoke is to see a man absolutely content with his career line.

The Cottage Handyman

Blessed are the handymen. Assuming we all have a bit of bird in us—I am, after all, tapping like a mad woodpecker at the moment—then the handyman, surely, is the great blue heron of cottage country. Like the majestic crane, handymen tend to be loners, often shy and territorial by nature, and rarely are two found on the same stretch of water. They also share an odd habit of standing perfectly still for long stretches, staring seemingly at nothing.

We are speaking, of course, of the Not-Always-Spotted Lake Handyman. And while there is no *Peterson Field Guide* to help with positive identification, there is a fairly generic description of this unusual species to be found in Margaret Laurence's *The Diviners:* "Royland looked the same as always. The same old bush jacket and beat-up trousers, the same grey beard as neatly trimmed as ever. The usual smile."

The fictional Royland of Laurence's Peterborough-area river was seventy-four years old, "too stubborn to wear glasses," and once explained his special gift of finding where to dig a well as "not something that everybody can do." The same applies, I suggest, to the many nonfictional Roylands who know how to lay a crib over ice in winter, hook up a jet pump, fell a hemlock so it doesn't take out the power lines, hang a door, level a sagging extension, fix a pilot light, mount a chimney, bleed a water tank, put up a deck without plans, and even, if necessary, fashion a cotter pin out of a rusty old nail.

These are special people. They are shared among lake dwellers like a secret family recipe. They could, if they so chose, easily get through an entire summer on other people's food and cold beer. They deal almost exclusively with those well enough off to have travelled to places where they will whine about "island time," without ever realizing that "lake time" is often slower. Yet no one here ever complains.

If cottagers sometimes seem overprotective of these patron saints of the backroads, it is both for selfish reasons— competition being dreaded at the lake at the same time as it is widely lamented in town—and for reasons that can only be described as humanitarian. These godsends tend to be scrupulously honest, but let us not pretend the economy of cottage country runs much the same way as the economy of the country. It's much more efficient, for one thing, with far less paperwork. Some handymen, in fact, have completely eliminated pesky paperwork altogether—refusing even to dirty their calloused fingers with a cheque. (I, of course, have receipts for everything, complete my quarterly GST filings, and invite PricewaterhouseCoopers up every Labour Day weekend for a barbecue and a forensic audit of the summer expenses—but I cannot speak for everyone.)

There is a different dynamic to cottage country work. It tends to get done, eventually, which is a considerable improvement over work that never gets done. Cottagers simply have to learn to be patient with the idiosyncrasies of this eccentric lot. Some jobs actually do require staring at for days on end before even the first footing can be set. Certain woodscrews do require individual trips to town.

Cottagers accept that, in the months of June, July, August, and September, it is necessary to take on three jobs for every one that can reasonably be done in the time allotted. Cottagers eventually learn to treat their handymen as absent-minded wanderers who emerge every so often from the bush, hammer a nail or two, stare awhile, and leave again.

By the time cottagers return to the cities to brag to coworkers how much they treasure the "rhythms" of the lake, they have already long forgotten the weeks they themselves stared out the back windows in the hopes that, finally, that old pickup truck would pull up with the last load of shingles.

I have often tried to figure out what power it is that these men hold over their summer captives. Many women think them "sexy," but this is baffling to another male, resplendent in his Eddie Bauers and sockless deck shoes, who sees only the frayed shirts, baggy pants, chafed workboots, sweat-lined hats, grey stubble, and thumbnails that sometimes look as if they also served as chisels. They not only carry no cellphone, they sometimes don't even have a phone! They can't talk about the stock market, never drive SUVs, and seem quite content to chitchat idly over a steaming cup of tea. Hardly the vision of the dynamic modern man.

Then again, they do know how things work, or why they don't work. And, unlike the rest of us, they know that, come tomorrow or the next day, if it isn't fixed, life goes on at its own sweet pace. Which we sometimes forget was the original draw of cottage country.

May 21

S M T W T F S
1
2 3 4 5 6 7 8
9 10 11 12 13 14 15
16 17 18 19 20 21 22
23 24 25 26 27 28 29
30 31

26°C. Hot and bright, not a cloud in the sky and hardly an empty space to be found in the government dock parking lot. It has changed overnight, the lake suddenly alive with boats and canoes. You can stand at the end of the dock and hear voices from the island.

The First Long Weekend

And so it has arrived. *Summer* begins this weekend—no matter what they tell you the official arrival is—and it will begin in different ways for different people who have headed out from towns to greet it. Perhaps the first sense of it will be the sound of a tent zipper, or a screen door bursting open on a cold and musty cottage. Perhaps it will be found in a broken cord on a flooded outboard or an empty can of bug spray, or seen in surprise sunburns the following day.

There will be fireworks this weekend, not because of some forgotten Queen, but because of remembered joy, because summer is here and we have suffered enough. It is time to trip the metabolism, time to ease up on the gas pedal, time to turn the daybook into kindling. It is time to leave the city and enter another country under other laws, where there are no judgments to be made against one who chooses to sit out in the sun with a cold beer for breakfast, where children may stay up as late as they are able, where ignorance is something to which we all aspire.

Somewhere out there is a place where there is no mail delivery at all, and no one complains. Somewhere out there is a place where the phone never rings, and no one sits by waiting. Somewhere out there is a place where there is no television, no replays, no highlights, and no one even to keep score.

What matters out there is not who's first in the polls, but who's first to fall in. What matters out there is not who is running for president or who will be the next prime minister or premier, but deadheads of another substance, only partially waterlogged. What matters out there is not government scandal or the latest drop in the stock market, but the price of Rapalas, the crispness of eight-month-old Corn Flakes, and a mutually agreeable volume on the portable CD player.

We all flee to different places, cottages with hot tubs and cottages with two-seaters, campgrounds with full electrical hookups and small clearings with a circle of rocks to contain the campfire. We come by air, by car, by inboard/outboard, by paddle, by foot. But however we get there, and wherever we go, there are the necessary rituals to go through.

There will be a walk to the raspberry patches, and while grand plans will be laid for pies once the bushes bloom and ripen, no raspberry will ever, in fact, make it out of the patch alive.

There will be a check along the shoreline for tadpoles and minnows, a check under the dock for the snapping turtle that collects a thousand missed heartbeats a year, a check in the bay just to make sure the sunken boat that has been there for thirty years will rot and roll and jangle small imaginations for at least one more.

There will be a paddle along the high rocks on the south shore in search of the majestic osprey that has not been seen now for two summers, but whose signature still stains white the outcropping where the best trout of the lake are invariably landed.

There will be an evening canoe ride down through the channel into a smaller lake still, where last year the usual family of three loons was four and where, this year, their return alone will be enough.

More than enough.

The First Swim

One of the nagging problems with great traditions is that they have this somewhat traditional habit of not living up to the past. Take the May 24th weekend for example. In memory the sun is always shining, the water calm, the blackflies out. There is lilac in the air, leaves on the trees, blisters on the top of your head. And a traditional May 24th weekend, of course, means the season's first quick dip—except, of course, when it's cold and raining.

But all winter you have looked forward to this weekend and the tradition it represents. We'll go swimming, you said in December, looking five months over the drifts. We'll go swimming, you said in March, looking two months beyond the muck. But then, like final exams and retirement, it all comes on you faster than expected.

Here it is already, the traditional May 24th weekend and you have followed all the traditional rules: packed the bathing suits and Deep Woods Off, driven five hours straight into the bush, marvelled at the cherry blossoms and wildflowers, and yet ... some years, despite all these best-laid plans, it feels like it might snow. The wind has turned, now coming out of the north, squalling on the water that traditionally is so calm and blue and inviting this precious weekend.

We haven't even finished with the docks. Every year since the invasion of the Visigoths, the docks here have been anchored, tied, and fixed with tightened bolts. The settling of the docks, unfortunately, also signals the first real dip, the splash that officially begins summer. Today, however, the temperature is far more double sweatshirt than bathing suit.

But the docks must be set. It's traditional. It takes an extra hour or more, but it can be done by lying flat on the dock and setting the pipes good enough for now. By the end, your hands are so numb all you can think of is running up and wrapping your arms around the wood stove. Except ... except that when you turn to run up, you are met by younger people in bathing suits, several of them shivering under the wrap of a thick beach towel.

"What are you doing?" you ask, as if you didn't know.

"Going swimming with you!"

"*I'm* not going in."

"You promised!"

You try a dozen different arguments, each one so filled with sense it seems impossible it does not work, but none of them do. Fifteen minutes later you discover your own bathing suit has somehow crawled up your pale, naked body and you are at the end of a dock, staring into the teeth of certain death.

"You *promised!*"

One after the other they have dropped off the end of the dock, scrambled out, and stand, now, shivering like new leaves in the wind while the ridiculous tradition is kept.

"You promised!"

Higher up, you hear a shout you have not heard since your grandmother was around to yell at your grandfather:

"You watch you don't have a heart attack!"

The dare issued, it must be taken. You drop off the dock, and it is as if the ice had not gone out, it had just gone under. Laughing forcibly, you take three quick, highly visible strokes for proof and leap from the water as if you had just noticed the cabin was on fire. You race up and in— hoping it is. Inside, you release the howl that you fought off while they were in hearing range. Behind you, the youngest stands at a bedroom door, pulling one sweatshirt over another, and laughing.

"Dad—why don't you just shut up about your stupid traditions."

I will, I will. Next year. And the year after.

The First Paddle

There is something about the firsts of the season we like
the best. First robin, first bike ride, first golf swing—for
this particular Canadian, first paddle. I cannot recall a
year in which it came so late, but perhaps there is something to that old theory about the longer the wait, the
greater the pleasure.

Up before the bugs, with the mist still hanging over the
far channel, I put in on water so smooth it seemed a shame
to crease it. There are days in this country when you
cannot help but feel like an invader. At this brief time of
year, the loons outnumber the people on this tiny lake on
the eastern edge of Ontario's Algonquin Park, and on a
crisp, cool spring day like this, even the dip of a paddle
seems an intrusion.

I set out, far too old to be still wishing I could paddle like
my mother—the paddle rarely leaving the water, the stroke
so gentle that it always seemed she was floating through the
air—but determined all the same not to disturb anything
that might be along the shore.

Sometimes, on a summer morning, you can come across
a cow moose feeding—on a lucky summer morning,

25

feeding with her new calf. There are times when you will find a large snapping turtle sunning in the bay that collects the driftwood (times as well when you will hear only the splash as it drops off the log, too quickly out of sight).

For the longest time, I could hear nothing but the dip of my own paddle and the slight gurgle of the keel as it sliced through flat water. No traffic in the distance, no planes overhead—the silence of the country as others found centuries ago in vehicles so similar to this one.

It taxes the mind to wonder why no sporting-goods giant has thought to reinvent the canoe—as they have with bicycles and cross-country skis—with a complete line of clothing and wraparound sunglasses to accompany it. But then, as I close in on shore again, all such ridiculous thoughts fade as the mind turns to the endless chirping of the red-eyed vireo, the bird likely least seen but most heard in this part of the country.

A half-century ago, on a lovely stretch of water north of here that runs east into the Upper Ottawa River, a woman named Louise de Kiriline Lawrence decided that she would count the number of times a day the single little vireo at her feeder sang. She rose at 5 A.M.—slightly earlier than I hit the water—and ticked off a total of 2155 songs in the first hour alone. By day's end, her count reached 22,197. A day's work for the little bird, but a walk in the park for Louise de Kiriline Lawrence, who had previously nursed the Dionne Quints and knew something about keeping track of the impossible.

I paddled down to the dam. So much water had fallen over the past weeks that it was lipping not only the dam itself but also the concrete retaining wall surrounding it, the lake like a pail in which someone had left a garden hose running. I checked for suckers at the bottom of the dam, but saw only the shadow of two or three as they darted in under the rocks.

On another late spring day, I had come down here with very small children and found more than a dozen of the pucker-mouthed fish sliced open and ripped in half, some partially eaten and some even still trying to swim about with fins missing and backs looking like they'd been raked by a propeller. There was no use making up a story. The kids knew instantly: a bear. And likely within an hour of our arrival.

It can be a violent country some days. Just as this day you could not imagine anything more gentle, the bush so quiet that even a toad moving across a dead leaf from last fall causes a walker to pause and wait until the sound comes again and the toad can be located.

I paddled back with a slight breeze beginning out of the north. So much has come out of the north lately—the wind, the air masses, the weather reports—that it has sometimes felt as if this spring had been bumped back, the wildflowers late, poplar stands just coming out in leaf, the bugs worse than the headlines.

But then came a noise rarely heard in these parts, the distant sound of arguing, or of a school letting out for recess—a sound that grew and grew until it seemed to fill the lake and all the high hills surrounding it. And then, gradually, the sound gave way to the sight of geese, a hundred or more of them rising over the last of the mist and then high over the trees.

Headed north, fortunately.

Late, but still ever so welcome.

May 30

S	M	T	W	T	F	S
						1
2	3	4	5	6	7	8
9	10	11	12	13	14	15
16	17	18	19	20	21	22
23	24	25	26	27	28	29
㉚	31					

21°C. Another still, lovely spring day. We tried to have a bonfire last night, but the bugs were terrible. Worst ever, someone said. They're always "worst ever." I wonder if anyone in this part of the world, at this time of the year, has ever said, "The bugs are good this year" or "great this year" or "the BEST ever."

Mosquitoes

Sometimes, when I lie here at night with the covers over my head, unable to sleep for the scratching and the slapping and the steady whine of miniature sirens in the air, I think that what this country needs is approximately one *billion* more cottagers.

This is not so far-fetched as it might sound. Edmund Collins, a 19th-century immigration promoter, once told the Canadian Club of New York that the Saskatchewan valley would easily be "capable of sustaining 800 million souls." So why not a population for Port Carling of, say, a mere 100 million, another 100 million for the Eastern Townships, 50 million for Lake Winnipeg, 100 million for the Alberta Foothills, 100 million for the B.C. Interior, 200 million for the Maritimes, 150 million for the northern reaches of the provinces and—seriously—the remaining 200 million just for Muskoka Road 8, where, this particular spring evening, the need is greatest?

The theory is simplicity itself. Everyone knows that China, with its billion law-abiding citizens, got rid of the housefly through government orders and government-issued fly swatters. So why can't we do the same for the irritating mosquito? And if it works there, why not the blackfly? The no-see-um? The deerfly? And that chainsaw-wielding, hair-burrowing, cruelly persistent and patient scourge of the August swim—the horsefly? Surely this poor, scratching country is deserving of a break after thousands of years of itching and slapping and calamine lotion.

The despised mosquito is as much a part of Canadian history as the rivers that brought the explorers into the heart of the country and the railroads that took the settlers to the West. John Cabot noted "Red Indians" in his log without realizing that he was seeing Natives who had, in desperation, smeared themselves with animal grease and red ochre in the hopes of fighting off the dreaded insects. A French Recollet brother travelling up the Ottawa River in the 1620s reported back to his superiors in France, "I confess that this is the worst martyrdom I suffered in this country." There is not a cottager anywhere who does not appreciate the depths of such sacrifice.

Bugs almost destroyed cottage country a century before there was a Weber's hamburger assembly line. "The black-flies and mosquitoes now made their appearance," Muskoka surveyor Vernon Wadsworth quickly scribbled in his journal in the early 1860s, "and in such swarms that we were badly bitten by them. I never saw such swarms of flies in all my six years' experience in the woods."

A few years later, when the first cottagers came up from, of all places, Pittsburgh, newcomers would cover themselves from head to foot in a ghastly mixture of pork and carbolic; the men would light smudge fires along the shore, but still the itching continued unabated.

Smudge pots, citronella candles, DDT, 6-12, Deep Woods Off, deet, Muskol, Avon Skin-So-Soft, ridiculous hats that make you look like a screened-in gazebo—nothing, absolutely nothing, seems to work.

All winter long we dream of opening up the cottage; all through the long drive we think of the work that will have to be done on the docks; the kids can hardly sit still for thinking about the exploring they will do—and fifteen minutes after arrival we are huddling in the kitchen while the cottage comes under attack from heat-seeking missiles. I check the cottage log and scratch my head (and a fresh bite) over the number of times someone has scribbled the phrase, *"The bugs have never been so bad!"*

There are approximately 100,000 species of insects in Canada. There are about 70 species of mosquito in this country, but 3000 that occur worldwide, many of them carrying the malaria-type diseases that make the mosquito a killer roughly equivalent to the asteroid that wiped out the dinosaurs. There are approximately 100 species of blackfly in Canada, but another 1500 or so can be found in other countries. We are, therefore, supposed to think ourselves relatively lucky when it comes to bugs.

Here, for those who need positive reinforcement at this time of year, are five critical points to consider:

- Only mossie females bite, so half our swatting is wasted energy.
- No bugs to drive the moose out to the side of the road, no photographs.
- No blackfly larvae in the streams, no food supply for the marvellous speckled trout we so treasure.
- No mosquitoes, no blackflies, no songbirds in cottage country.
- No blackflies to do the pollinating, no blueberry crop, no pies.

That being said, there are pies and trout at the grocery store, there are dozens of CDs of bird songs, and Larry's little store at the end of the road has a good supply of post-cards of Algonquin moose. But on a night like this, huddling under the covers, the negatives so outweigh the positives that another few million cottagers on this little lake actually seems to make sense.

So long as I could sleep through the racket of everyone slapping.

June 12

S	M	T	W	T	F	S
			1	2	3	4
5	6	7	8	9	10	11
13	14	15	16	17	18	19
20	21	22	23	24	25	26
27	28	29	30			

12°C. Slight north wind. A good many changes since last trip. There are two hemlocks down by the road. My father spent all his life in logging and always said the tree he trusted least was the hemlock. I know why. They have almost no root and can break off at any time. Fortunately, no harm done—not like that other time—and we can always burn the wood.

The Power
of Nature

All I had to do to see the power of nature was step out the door: the cabin next door had been squashed. A week ago, the wind had reared up out of the east, blown down our bay, and knocked one large hemlock onto the little sleeping cabin, destroying it beyond repair, and had toppled another smaller hemlock onto the roof of the slightly larger cabin, ripping off a large portion of the shingles.

Then, only days later, just as the roofers had finished the new shingling, it happened again. In a coincidence that defies comprehension, a freak windstorm roared this time out of the west and snapped off an even larger hemlock that crumpled down onto the new roof and squashed the cabin as surely as if the heel of a workboot had been slammed into an empty pop tin.

Those who had been working on the property were lucky to escape with their lives. One man, who had spent much of the night in hospital being monitored for shock, had described the arriving wind like "a train coming through a tunnel" when it hit—a curious description to hear in a place where people go for the peace and only on certain nights when the wind is right can you even hear the logging truck moving down distant Highway 60.

This is the time of year when Canadians open up their doors and head out into a world that both welcomed and terrified their ancestors. The lake invites; the lake takes. The sky is magical; the sky is threatening. We welcome a breeze; we fear the wind.

In Saskatchewan a few days after the cabin next door had been destroyed, a tornado touched down south of Regina and several other funnel clouds were spotted across the province. On Vancouver Island, an eight-year-old girl was attacked by a cougar while on a kayaking tour with her parents, and though the kayakers beat off the animal in time, everyone who heard this tale and the others knew that there would be other such stories before the best season ended, and would invariably express shock at how quickly the unexpected can happen. "Nature, as we know her," said Thoreau, "is no saint."

It was quiet at the lake in the days following the windstorm. There were still three weeks left before school would let out. The fogs were heavy, the high water from the rain had logs floating freely, but there were, fortunately, no scurrying boats filled with children to worry about. The silence felt odd, particularly when I went to stand, as I did several times, and stare in disbelief at the destruction brought about by a huge hemlock that decided, after three centuries of standing free, simply to break off like a tulip and drop to the ground.

I keep a slim book on the cabin shelf, *A Life in the Country,* in which my great hero in journalism, Bruce Hutchison, correctly argues that "No one ever owns a cabin or an acre of forest, whatever the title deeds in the land registry may say. We were transient tenants to be quickly forgotten like our predecessors, Indian and White. But the forest lived on, perpetually renewing itself."

It was something worth considering when, coming back along the path, my daughter Christine and I stumbled across two exquisite pink lady's slippers—the delicate wild orchid of these parts—and realized that the wildflowers had risen exactly where the workers ran as they hurried to escape the falling tree.

It doesn't matter the day or the weather—all I have to do to see the astonishing power of nature is step out the door. A hemlock goes down; an orchid rises. And we stand in awe of both.

June 18

S M T W T F S
~~1~~ ~~2~~ ~~3~~ ~~4~~ ~~5~~
~~6~~ ~~7~~ ~~8~~ ~~9~~ ~~10~~ ~~11~~ ~~12~~
~~13~~ ~~14~~ ~~15~~ ~~16~~ ~~17~~ (18) 19
20 21 22 23 24 25 26
27 28 29 30

21° C. Cloudy with the odd sunny break. Easy ride over—little traffic in either direction. Stopped a couple of times for the old dog to stretch her legs and once for a bear cub that was running along the side of the road near the logging museum and couldn't seem to decide whether or not to cross. No sign of a mother—hope nothing happened to her. Three moose, as well. Two in the bog just beyond Cache Lake. The other, naturally, in its usual spot near the Rock Lake turnoff.

The Ministry Moose

There are several theories about the Ministry Moose. She stands, ankle deep in muck, just to the east of the Rock Lake turnoff at approximately the centre of the Highway 60 corridor through Algonquin Park.

The Ministry Moose—so named by a cousin who grew increasingly suspicious concerning the regular hours she appears to keep—sometimes stands on the north side of the road, sometimes on the south, but always within camera range of the passing tourists who stop. She pays no attention to their coming and going. She sometimes munches the grasses, sometimes wades out into the shallow water and feasts on water lily, but always, always, seems to be there when we pass by on the way to the cottage.

There is some thought that she is a mechanical contraption placed there at first light and taken away at dusk by the Ministry of Natural Resources. The Ministry, understandably, is keen not to disappoint tourists who may come from as far away as Japan to see a Canadian moose in the wild. There is another school of thought that the moose is a devilishly clever costume worn by a couple of junior rangers whose summer task is to play the moose, but there is something about the impossibly skinny ankles that made me doubt this. I suspect, rather, that the Ministry Moose is merely a regular—one of so many in our fair-weather lives.

Those who do not know the pleasures of returning year after year to the same summer retreat presume, correctly, that the first thing we do on arrival is check the pantry for mice, the dock for ice damage, and the water pump for leaks. We do all of these things, of course, but we also check the sky for the osprey, the isolated bay at the foot of the lake for nesting loons, and under the dock for Snappy.

It would not be summer if the big snapping turtle did not show up early on to greet us, drifting off the end of the dock like an astronaut on a space walk as he—more likely *she*—stares straight up at us before suddenly turning and vanishing back into the dark of the deeper waters with our imaginations. We take joy from these sightings—even of the old turtle—for it is proof that they, too, have survived the winter. We look for the ruffed grouse and her chicks, the fox and her kits, the old bear at the dump who may have a new cub.

They are also our neighbours. And, over time, you get to know them as well as, sometimes better than, neighbours who drive up rather than merely show up. They have their own characteristics, their own quirks, their own ways about them. There is, for example, a lovely, sleek fox who comes to sit by the campfire whenever one of us happens to be there without the dog. There is a chipmunk who will take peanuts out of your pocket, and a squirrel more critical than Her Majesty's Loyal Opposition.

When she lived year round in the Park, our grandmother attracted deer the way other eccentric older women sometimes surround themselves with pigeons or cats. She put out salt licks and broke up dried bread loaves, and they would gather outside her log home as regularly as if the mill whistle had just blown to signal lunch. There was one special deer, Sugar, who was so close to our grandmother that it seemed, at times, as if they were standing by the woodpile passing the time of day. Each spring Sugar would *present* her fawn—sometimes two—for the old girl's approval, and the moment would be marked with sugar cubes and congratulations. It was a deep friendship that went on for more than a dozen years. The day we found Sugar at the side of the road, dead from a collision with a lumber truck, was as if a family member had died. And in a way, one had.

It is not a perfect world we humans invade each summer. Childhood curiosity alone exacts a heavy price among the minnows and toads and other creepy-crawlies that are so much a part of the cottage experience. One trusts, however, that the damage will be minimized by those who once learned better themselves, and that respect is something that can be handed down as effectively as love for a particular place.

We have our little jokes about the Ministry Moose. We imagine her rusting out, or the battery dying. And yet, if she were not there, regular as a punched clock, we would not be there, either—for something significant in our lives would be missing.

Crokinole

It came out of the blue—the way the best calls do. The caller wished to know if anyone here had any use for an old crokinole board. It had, she said, once been in a cabin in New Brunswick, later in a small cottage in the Ontario bush, but now there was no more cottage and she did not know what to do with the old board.

Her husband had died, much too young, and the rustic place in the country had been sold. She was on the verge, she said, of tossing the game out when she thought she'd take a chance and just see if it might have one more life left in it. "You've got kids," she said. "And you sometimes write about being at the lake—would you like to have it?" She was offering it free. She did not even know us. She merely hoped that another generation might pick up something that she and her husband had always enjoyed on those quiet evenings when the television reception is particularly bad for the very good reason that there is neither reception nor television.

The game is not complicated and takes up very few bytes of the human brain. Players in turn take shots, using their fingers to flick the men—or discs, as the aficionado prefers—into scoring position or else to take out the opposition. It is played on a round board surrounded by an octagonal frame with a slightly raised brim to keep in the stray shots. The board is often homemade, usually of plywood and lots of varnish, and there are annoying pegs protecting the inner circle, where, if one of your discs happens to land by design or fluke, you are then granted permission to yell and scream and gloat and drive younger brothers and sisters to tears.

There is also something wonderfully Canadian about this simple board game. It came out of rural Canada around the time of Confederation—the World Championship is held each year in Tavistock, Ontario—which would give it an earlier claim on the national psyche than hockey. Perhaps it's just as well, though, that it never became the national game. Otherwise we'd be seeing television ads aimed at boorish parental behaviour at crokinole tournaments.

The two games, however, do have a connection in that "crokinole finger" is a condition caused, medical experts believe, by the Canadian tendency to believe it is possible to take a slapshot by violently flicking the middle finger into one of the small wooden discs, which, admittedly, do slightly resemble hockey pucks.

It was the wooden discs, in fact, that ultimately led me to Toys "R" Us. I had picked up the crokinole board—homemade, highly varnished, in perfect shape—and was on my way home when I realized this board had all its wooden discs in perfect order (twelve black, twelve pale) and was, therefore, far superior to the old board at the lake, with its misfit collection of red and white "checkers." If we had two sets of proper discs, we could have tournaments, two games running simultaneously—the Wimbledon of crokinole.

Toys "R" Us is a massive toy store a friend once called "Disneyland for poor people," where, on a slow Sunday afternoon, he would unleash his two toddlers like puppies in a park until they were tired enough to pass out. I figured if anyone would have the discs it would be there.

It is a strange experience to go into a large toy store once you have fallen out of touch with Christmas wishlists. Many of the new toys are simply ludicrous—the kid's "automatic golf cart" at $19.99, the remote-control car worth more than the vehicle I had just left in the parking lot—but some of them are unexpectedly old.

This is, according to the marketing experts, the third Christmas in a row where the theme has been "retro"—a return to the past highlighted by the likes of Lego. Everything old is suddenly new again. One whole wall contains G.I. Joe—the number one wish of my younger brother nearly forty years ago. Joe has, of course, been repackaged to suit the times: one attack package is called "Sites on Baghdad." A touch of retro can also be found in the massive games section, once you work your way past the video game stacks and find the shelf containing tiddly-winks, pick-up sticks, and checkers. I was getting close.

"Can I help you?"

I turned. The woman in charge of games was smiling.

"Crokinole," I said.

"What?"

"Crokinole," I repeated. "The board game. I need some discs."

"Croke?"

"Crokinole," I repeated one more time.

"I've never heard of it—is it a game?"

Not only a game, ma'am, but as retro as it gets.

And, if I may, as *Canadian* as the national game itself.

June 25

S M T W T F S
1 2 3 4 5
6 7 8 9 10 11 12
13 14 15 16 17 18 19
20 21 22 23 24 (25) 26
27 28 29 30

25°C. Bright and still. They say "school lets out," but I've never heard "the lake lets in." Yet it's almost as if a door opens between the two, school and the lake, and in an instant the sound of the schoolyard becomes the sound of the lake. There are those who do not like it when the young families invade the quiet of the lake, but I love it. To me, the sound of children's voices carrying across the water is as much a part of summer as the wind in the high pines.

The Lure of Summer

Strange, isn't it, how we say seasons arrive when, for most Canadians, summer is the one we go to? Perhaps this is because the Canadian summer is less season than state, and much more than state of mind because it is, somehow, both state of being and state of *not*-being at the same time.

The true northern "summer" does not lie, as the calendar suggests, between June 21 and September 21, give or take a few inexplicable hours in either direction. It is, rather, found, in weekend cheats and two- and three-week stretches, early May to early October. And it exists—as the photographs we get back in the late fall will mysteriously show—solely under blue skies and over calm water, and far more often at sunset than at any other time of day.

In our case, we left a city of more than a million other Canadians and, over the final few minutes of gravel ruts, mudholes, and fallen branches, passed the only other Canadians in the immediate vicinity: three small foxes and a rather alarmed ruffed grouse. Radio reception had died before the pavement gave out. There was, at this point I am writing about, no running water apart from kids racing down to the lake with empty buckets and back with full.

The docks had once again been knocked silly by fluctuating water levels and a recent windstorm. The blackflies were still out. There was thunder sounding from the east. The water was cold for the time of year. And the outhouse needed moving or digging out—soon. Yet we could not be happier.

It is hard, even for one Canadian to another, to explain the lure of the northern summer. In David Macfarlane's lovely 1999 novel, *Summer Gone,* he writes of a saying that, somewhere, is painted on the rafters of a camp dining hall: "Summer is the stillness between things." It is such a charming thought, for it is this stillness, this pause amid the madness, this hiatus in life, this sabbatical from reality, that we all seek and ever more desperately need.

Each of us has that one special place where time does indeed seem to slow, if not quite stop. For us, it is here along the south shore of this deep, cold lake on the edge of Ontario's Algonquin Park. But it could as easily be the Queen Charlotte Islands, the mountains around Jasper, the lonely lakes and rivers of northern Saskatchewan and Manitoba, the Laurentians, the Restigouche, Cape Breton Island, Cavendish, L'Anse aux Meadows, or a thousand other well-known or secret getaways across the country.

It could also be heading out to a favourite campsite or small-town home or the family farm, perhaps for a family reunion. It could, for that matter, also be just sitting all alone, with a cool drink and a warm book, in the backyard, where, when the conditions are just right, the magical Canadian summer can be as good as it gets.

We Canadians are often self-deprecating to the point of injury, but it is not so with our summer, which we hold to be the equal of, or better than, anyone else's season anywhere on this Earth. We feel much as Stephen Leacock felt as the *Mariposa Belle* was about to set out in the morning sunlight of Lake Wissanotti, with the long call of the loon echoing and the air cool and fresh. "Don't talk to me of the Italian lakes, or the Tyrol or the Swiss Alps," Leacock wrote. "Take them away. Move them somewhere else. I don't want them."

There is a value Canadians put on their summer that sometimes defies even logic. Every once in a while a bureaucrat or a testy writer of letters to the editor will push for year-round schooling on the excellent grounds that summers off make for poor use of facilities and that education and teaching should be continual concerns, not just ten-month commitments. But that argument never goes anywhere for the very good reason that most Canadians believe summer to be its own course, and a mandatory one for their children. Fiscal sense, in a country where doors are closed more than half the year, does not always make good psychological sense.

It may be that we treasure summer so much because it is so fleeting. We speak of summer romance and summer friends as if they were never intended to last. We treat it as our own secret time, those few precious weeks when we believe we have somehow mastered the trick of living two lives.

Timing is everything at this point of the year. There are only a few days when the blueberries are perfect, even fewer when the flax is in bloom. The second cut of hay has its peak moment just as, later in August, in one week that comes upon us far too quickly, the water will turn and no longer carry those surprising currents of warmth.

When summer seems slightly late, it can cause an anxiety out of all proportion to the actual date. It is the last week of June *and the days are getting shorter!* Such worry is nothing new for Canadians: "The short Canadian summer," the poet Wilfred W. Campbell wrote in 1907, "Whose every lonesome breath / Holds hints of autumn and winter, / As life holds hints of death."

This, however, is not 1907, and summer has taken on a new role as the one opportunity each of us has for doing absolutely nothing—something that has become far more difficult today than it ever was in the day of Wilfred W. Campbell. The turning of the millennium was—at least according to the science magazines of the 1950s—supposed to herald a new era in which leisure time would, finally, outstrip work time, when we would have more time off than on, when all the work of the past century would deliver, in the new century, a time unlike that ever before known in history.

In 1983, this is how the British secretary of energy, Peter Walker, saw the future unfolding: "We have the opportunity of creating Athens without the slaves, where the slaves will be the computer and the microchip, and the human race can obtain a new sense of enjoyment, leisure and fulfillment."

Athens without the slaves. This is what computer programs, networking, email, and cellphones would bring us all. Instead, technology has made slaves of us all, tied twenty-four hours a day to work, reachable anywhere at any time for any imaginable or unimaginable reason. The fact is that leisure time has not grown, it has shrunk. In many cases, severely.

All of which is to say that this surprising development in social values and commitment has had the effect of making summer, and escape, all the more valued. There are still in this vast country, mercifully, places where cellphones are far out of range, places where there are no plugs for computers or phone lines for modems, places where telephones do not ring, meetings are not held, and deadlines are set, if at all, by the sun's position in the sky. We do not think of it as "Athens without the slaves," yet if it were "Canada without the mosquitoes," we would call it paradise indeed.

But the bugs be damned. The sun has just broken through here on the edge of Algonquin Park.

It is time to take the first swing off the long rope that hangs from the yellow birch at the edge of the shore, one long swing out over the lake and one endless, timeless drop into that which will wash away everything—winter, job, worries, even age—that has built up in the too-long time between who we have to be and who we'd like to be.

Ourselves, with summer just beginning.

The "Stupid Stop"

The "Stupid Stop" was possibly not my own invention—I don't really care who invented it, just that it exists—but I did name it, and I like to suppose that it will outlast me. After all, it is a quarter-century or more since we started making them—so the Stupid Stop is as much a cottage tradition by now as the snapping turtle gliding by the end of the dock like some unexpected, yet annual, apparition.

Nothing ever comes of the turtle. Kids run; he or she runs; and summer slips on. But the snapper reminds them of where they are, just as the Stupid Stop always prepares them for where they are headed: the cottage, which is not at all the same as home.

The Stop was always the halfway point of the drive—in this case the small town of Barry's Bay—and the Stupid part was all mine. The kids would each get a dollar or two, once in a blue moon a five-dollar bill, and a half-hour to spend it on something absolutely useless. Money deliberately to be spent in one place—and by no means wisely.

All those years of stupidity added up to some of the most useless items known to childkind: bulbous plastic rings, miniature card decks, broken balsa gliders, potato guns, suction-cup darts, doll jewellery, caps, miniature folding scissors, rubber snakes, spiders, and tiny, hard-plastic dolls with their legs missing. Useless, obviously, but they served a purpose: to remind all that, at the cottage, different rules apply.

This summer, with all of them now in their twenties, they arrived with everything from mechanical bubble blowers to water guns to a three-man slingshot that could land a water balloon on the far island if only I'd let them fire it. I told them not to, then immediately went indoors, out of sight and, presumably, out of mind. I later found dozens of tiny burst balloons stretching from the deck to the dock. I did not check the far island, but I wouldn't be surprised.

I don't think fun gets the respect it requires, even more so than it deserves. These now-grown children—and, presumably, their children to come—all come from modern suburbia, a world where life runs in sixty-minute cycles, fifty minutes if a Zamboni is involved. They come from a culture in which idle time is as deeply mistrusted as strangers. They come from a world where "fun" is a word parents use for hockey practices, gymnastics, diving, tae kwon do, Brownies, ballet, baseball, soccer, swimming, and art.

Generally speaking, if you're getting yelled at to hurry out to an ice-cold car, racing somewhere while a parent tells you how much this is costing, getting yelled at while you're there, and often getting yelled at again on the way home, you are supposedly having a good time in the 21st century. This makes it somewhat difficult for a modern child to have fun at a cottage, where cars are usually too hot to get into and where no one goes anywhere anyway.

What the Stupid Stop does is put responsibility—as well as a welcome dash of irresponsibility—back into the hands of children. They can do with their Stupid money what they like just as, once they reach the cottage, they're welcome to make their own decisions on how to spend their time. Their biggest problem, obviously, is fighting off the one parent (pleased to meet you) who simply cannot help himself when it comes to organizing everyone else's life.

But I learned a lesson a few years ago when I picked up a used crokinole board at a flea market and took it back to the city with fantasies of the kids sitting around playing on a winter's night, just as they so often do at the cottage in the summer. They never once touched it. I think they resented its presence in a world where it does not belong.

Strange isn't it, but in the city, where they have Super Nintendo, cellphones, DVDs, and MP3s, the young complain constantly about boredom. At the cottage, there is the lake, the old fishing boat, a washtub that's perfect for toads and salamanders, fungus to draw on, lures to dive for, canoes to tip, and—increasingly as the children grew older—a nightly fire where they could sit with their friends and talk until even the loons fell asleep.

I remember once asking the youngest what he liked best about the cottage. "I'm never bored," he answered. His older sisters once took some Stupid Stop money and bought a thick rope that they tied to the top of the old yellow birch that hangs out over the water. They cleared a runway and tied a knot to get a grip on, and for twelve years now that rope has been the family entertainment centre of the cottage. And sometimes, when things get a bit slow, one of them will scream "Snapping turtle!" just as someone has reached the end of the swing and is about to drop into the water.

Stupid, but too late to stop. Which is why, under the different rules by which a cottage operates, it's brilliant.

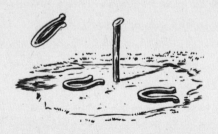

June 27

S	M	T	W	T	F	S
	1	2	3	4	5
6	7	8	9	10	11	12
13	14	15	16	17	18	19
20	21	22	23	24	25	26
(27)	28	29	30

18°C. Still cool, wind still out of the north, throwing a chill on matters. It's sweater weather, not swimsuit. The government parking lot has been thinning out all week long as families bail. There's a theory in town that if summer doesn't "happen" by the 15th of July, it ain't gonna happen. Silly, of course, but it makes the point. When you're dealing with a precious commodity like time off, you can't leave much to chance—not even weather. Those who decided to "park" their holidays until August are probably laughing.

July versus August

Welcome to The Great Canadian Debate. Not federal versus provincial, French versus English, East versus West— or even Tim Hortons versus Starbucks. But July versus August. We speak of "summer" as if it were a single, glorious moment, but summer, like winter, has many different faces, some far more attractive than others—and we generally break our favourite season down to the two holiday months, July and August. They may both be summer, but they are far from twins.

I speak as one who has changed allegiance. For many years, especially when the children were small, we were a "July" family, booking, whenever possible, whatever time we could get as close to the Canada Day weekend as possible. Summer escape could never come fast enough. Several years back, however, I was forced to switch to August, by dint of being assigned by my newspaper to cover the 1996 Atlanta Olympics, and have never looked back. We are now, and likely ever will be, an "August" family, treasuring our summer weeks the way a child will sometimes hoard candy—the wait and the sure knowledge that it is coming almost as delicious as the chewing itself.

Let us list, then, the factors in favour of July—at least of most Julys:

- Summer has arrived, and why risk missing the best days of it?
- There is a glorious, extravagant sense that the holidays are just beginning and, in the eyes of a child, will go on forever.
- There is more daylight—time enough, even, to get eighteen holes in at the twilight fee.
- There is a sense of newness: new toys for the water, new people on the lake, new bestsellers by the hammock, new projects—for those who *must*—for the cottage.
- You will have an early tan that should last the summer.
- You can sense the water getting warmer each time you dive off the end of the dock.
- The strawberries are finishing up, the raspberries out, the blueberries coming.
- The baby loons are learning to dive, an act someone once compared to dunking ping pong balls.
- Kids, who control just about everything else in your life, are impossible if you do not get them to the lake immediately on school letting out.
- Your friends are going to be there in July—so how can you not be there?

- The locals are happy to see you. Or at least seem to be.
- Summer still isn't over—there are, after all, still two long weekends to go—unlike the end of August, which feels like the first Sunday of the year: responsibility looming.

August, on the other hand, is hardly without its fan club:

- The corn and tomatoes are ripe, and cheap, at the road stops on the way to the lake.
- The bugs are much improved. The blackflies are gone, the mosquitoes reduced, and, if we could only get rid of that horsefly that lands on your head every time you surface from a dive, outside would be paradise defined.
- The evenings are shorter and slightly cooler, making campfires last longer and matter more.
- The water is perfect.
- The overpriced stuff of July is on sale.
- There are sometimes meteor showers on clear nights.
- The lake is quieter and the town less crowded.
- You can gloat over those who have already spent their holidays—like the bond holder grinning at the investor who went with high-tech, or the one who set aside dessert for a bed-time snack.

There is, for the August holidayer, a feeling that summer is truly over, not continuing on without you, and that you may as well return to jobs and schools and start signing the kids up for all those spare moments they are about to lose.

It is an intriguing debate without clear resolution. Those who choose July believe they savour the best of summer; those who pick August believe they get pieces of July anyway and get a prolonged satisfaction out of denial.

Some insist on July; some swear by August; and some, like us, flip flop from one to the other and may, before too long, flop back again, convinced that one month holds one more ray of sunshine than the other.

Some others, we feel obliged to point out, are just as happy to let us argue the merits of one over the other. They go with September. When the rest of us go home and the lake quiets down again. When fires and morning coffee and mist on the water and long walks together take on a whole new meaning.

And when the first streaks of red in the maples are a reminder of the passing of the best summer ever—with even better ones yet to come.

July 1

S	M	T	W	T	F	S
				①	2	3
4	5	6	7	8	9	10
11	12	13	14	15	16	17
18	19	20	21	22	23	24
25	26	27	28	29	30	31

23°C. Still and quiet this morning, a ghostly mist running the narrows between the far island and the dam. I went for a dawn paddle, so quiet, so lovely, trout surfacing over the shoals and a pair of baby loons in the hidden bay at the far end of the lake. The sunrise was glorious, almost like bright paint dripping down from the hills. So unbelievably quiet, the day so full of promise and possibilities. There's a sense on a day like this that the year is just beginning and, as we all once felt as kids, will never, ever come to an end.

Canada Day

This is where I come to celebrate Canada Day. This is the place where I like my country best. Please understand: none of this is intended as anything against those who gathered on Parliament Hill or took part in small-town bike rallies or put on a local fireworks show for the neighbourhood children. I have been on the Hill in past years and gloried in it, and have watched pyrotechnic displays with small children in my arms and loved it. But, given my druthers, I'll take an early morning canoe ride through the mist any day, Canada Day included.

I can make it sound perfectly idyllic, or I can tell the truth. Part of this particular Canada Day involved replacing a rotted wall in the outhouse that was built somewhere around Centennial Year and, in hot weather, has been known to get higher than the fireworks display over the Peace Tower. Part required the bailing out of an old tin boat I had forgotten to haul up and flip over the last time here. And part, as well, included the clearing out of squirrel and mouse nests in the old shed where the paddles are kept—as well as a late evening attack on a burgeoning hornets' nest with a tall, pressurized can that, in these parts, qualifies as a weapon of mass destruction.

But I must also tell you that my Canada Day included a swim in water so clear and clean and cold that there are those here—just as there are Canadians in many other parts of this fortunate country—who still drink it straight from the lake. There are those who say that in the future water will become the most valued resource in our country. I think an argument can be made that it has always been.

And my Canada Day also included a swing and a long, lazy flip off a thick rope that is tied to a birch limb and leaves you, momentarily suspended, high over the water with no other choice but to drop. I may have finally reached an age where I no longer care if anyone watches, but not such an age where swinging off a rope into the lake no longer matters.

On my Canada Day, I do not sit around, as one beer company might wish to think, wondering which prime minister I might like to share a cold one with—but I do wonder each year if the Unknown Camper has made it in yet to his secret campsite. Not many miles from here there is an old, abandoned logging road. And for those with nothing better to do on an early summer's day, it is possible to walk in a mile or two over fallen trees to an old corduroy road that will take you through a swamp, where, at this time of year, the snapping turtles will have laid their eggs and the fox and raccoon have usually already feasted on them.

For those few who know precisely where to turn off the rough logging road, there is a spruce stand that gives way to an even rougher trail that twists and turns and at times even vanishes over fallen trees and slippery moss to a small creek that tends to go dry by midsummer. The proper turn at this creek, however, will take you in through a hardwood forest and over a small knoll to a rocky outcropping that runs along a lake so small no one has ever properly got around to naming it.

I came here the first time by accident, walking along the creek bed to see if it led to a larger body of water. It did, but only larger in the way a pail is bigger than a glass. There was, however, something here far more quickening to the imagination than a dark, untapped pool of brook trout. The rocky outcropping led to a campsite that, it seemed, had just been swept and polished. There was a canoe tucked in under a cedar tree. A small stone campfire with a makeshift wind wall sat just up from the water. And down by the low rocks, the Unknown Camper had rolled a large log into such a position that if you sat there and waited, the sun would seem to set in your lap.

On the high rocks, well removed from the campsite and the smoothed-over pine needles where he would raise his tent, the view was better positioned for the sunrise—and here he had built an elaborate outdoor toilet to greet the new day in his own glory.

I go there often, but have never seen him, either standing or sitting. And I could say I checked to see if he was there on this special day. But I deliberately did not check in case he was there. For Canada Day is not always about crowds, public places, and loud celebration. It is also about private places. And quiet reflection.

Cottage Reading

Think of it as the human equivalent of a radiator flush. We are talking here about the lost art of turning off, tuning out, and dropping away for a while.

My holidays begin this week. I prefer not to say when they will end, for it is an admission that they will, indeed, one day come to end. I'd rather fool myself in thinking summer lasts forever. This is the best feeling, and one I seem to need. I am hardly alone in this. "Every so often," Colorado naturalist John A. Murray once said, "a disappearance is in order." He called it a "vanishing," a "checking out," an "indeterminate period of unavailability." In other words, don't call.

I can sense this "disappearance" beginning the moment we turn onto that single-lane dirt path where the raspberry bushes run along the paint job like a nail on a blackboard: the first sign you're waking up to the world you prefer to be in. The physical trappings are easily described: a cabin, a lake, an outhouse, a washtub filled with toads. The psychological trappings are less easily detailed, for it is their absence that so delights: No television. No newspaper. No magazine racks. No radio except for the weather and, on mornings when the flesh is weak, last night's baseball scores.

For one who works in news and has, in what seems now the very distant past, been at one point so psychologically deranged that he could recite the salient points of the Meech Lake Accord without pausing for breath, this sensory deprivation is the spiritual equivalent of being born again. That does not mean reading is prohibited. On the contrary, reading is encouraged. It is just, well, the type of reading that changes. Not the *New York Times* or the *Times of London,* but the *Weekly World News,* with exclusive and inspirational photos of evil children who have been sent by their parents to "live on an island of the damned!" Not *Maclean's,* but the *National Enquirer,* where we learn for the first time of the "terrifying, mysterious illness" that has stricken Cher. Would *Maclean's* tell us that scientists may be on the verge of crossing chickens with pigs to produce bacon-flavoured eggs? I don't think so.

There is no shame in being out of touch. The readers of the year-old *Ladies' Home Journal* that sits on the night table have just voted on their favourite television shows, and *I Love Lucy,* which left in 1962, was number one, followed by *M.A.S.H.,* which stopped production in 1983. Who would argue?

I spend so much of my work life reading for necessity it is sometimes hard to adjust back to reading for pleasure, for pure delight. I sometimes have to remind myself of the words of James Boswell, the author of *Life of Johnson,* who said more than two centuries back that "A man ought to read just as inclination leads him—for what he reads as a task will do him little good."

I have long been bemused by those early summer newspaper surveys of what the literary crowd is reading. I have always imagined them scurrying about the internet and the library shelves to come up with whatever obscure South American novelist or Bulgarian diarist is going to make them look far more worldly and brighter than they in fact are. We wait in vain for the day one of them has the self-assurance to admit to a grocery-store bestseller, a thriller, or an old-fashioned mystery—the literary truths of a summer well spent.

I take pride in my lack of summer sophistication. I read comic books, mysteries, the grocery-line scandal sheets, even the backs of cereal boxes. And I do so happily knowing that at least once each summer I shall assuage whatever guilt needn't be felt by including one worthy in my reading. Not *War and Peace,* not *Ulysses,* but a book that is no chore at all to read and yet makes a reader feel the equivalent of a procrastinating tinkerer who has finally fixed the steps down to the dock or dug a new hole for the outhouse.

This quirk may well be genetic. My father lived his life deep in the bush and read constantly: *Police Gazette* one evening, Plutarch the next. Living back in the bush, he could not possibly have read for "show." He read not for other people but for himself, and it is a lesson worth keeping to. I read whatever I feel like, including a handful of worthies a season. The rules are simple: The book must be older than I am and the author must be dead.

We read as children by coal oil lamp and, after the lamp was blown out, by flashlight, and all four of us ended up with thick glasses, but also with an overload of arcane knowledge. *Want to know the Beagle Boys' prison numbers? The janitor's name at Riverdale High? Where Green Lantern got his power?* Yet it also left us all readers, and even if we did begin with Archie and Richie Rich and, yes, Sgt. Rock, we did begin somewhere and we have all somehow ended up with the appropriate hardcover habits to get one through a dinner party.

But not come summer. Come summer, I still read for myself. The coal oil light has gone electric and, since I am now the parent, the flashlight is unnecessary; yet there is still that same precious delight that comes to the printed word only when there is also rain on the roof, a loon on the lake, and the smells of canvas, cedar, and mosquito repellent in the air.

It is also easier at the cottage to keep up with the past than with the latest news, and we have developed an odd pleasure in learning again what has been long forgotten.

On a rough shelf in this particular cabin, for example, is an August 1963 *Reader's Digest* in which Lester Pearson says: "I am not concerned with power for the sake of pomp or power." There is also a *Maclean's* from March 1969 in which astonishment is expressed at how much professional athletes are making, people like Gordie Howe hauling in $65,000 a year and Russ Jackson getting $30,000 a year just to make sure Ottawa has a respectable football team.

The best reading of all, however, is to be found in an April 1969 edition of *Popular Mechanics*. In the section called "Just Patented: PM's Pick of the New Inventions," we are advised that very shortly we will be enjoying:

- foam foundations
- walk-in bathtubs
- muscle-powered fishing motors
- emergency brakes that drop down into the pavement and catapult the car into the air.

Nearly forty years later, we're still waiting. Who knows? Forty years from now we may still be waiting for bacon-flavoured eggs. Not to mention—sorry, I can't resist—for the Toronto Maple Leafs to win the Stanley Cup. That's what rediscovering perspective is all about.

July 10

S	M	T	W	T	F	S
				1	2	3
4	5	6	7	8	9	(10)
11	12	13	14	15	16	17
18	19	20	21	22	23	24
25	26	27	28	29	30	31

Lovely today—summer has returned! Thermometer hit 27°C by 10 A.M. Saw merganser and thirteen little ones parade by the dock in perfect order, each one going over the same floating log in exactly the same tumble-down manner. A perfect day for loafing. Nothing scheduled but a trip to the dump— and a nap.

The Cottage Dump

For a diminishing number of us, a cottage is not an investment, but a collection of experiences. And one of the very sweetest has been taken away. We can't even say we're down in the dumps about it—because in the dump is precisely where we want to be.

Just look around. Water is boiling in the kettle. Bread is in the toaster. I am sitting in a chair that lists toward the water. All three—kettle, toaster, chair—were summer gifts picked up by my father-in-law, a retired schoolteacher who is, unfortunately, no longer with us. But if he were, he would discover he could no longer partake in what was once his favourite pastime: touring the summer garbage dumps. He would need to find another hobby, and I doubt he could come up with one he would enjoy half as much. Certainly not one that could furnish his cottage for free.

A few years back, the authorities threw padlocks on the gates and nailed up "No Trespassing" signs. The old landfill sites, as they prefer to call their dumps, were legally closed to the public, declared environmental hazards. The few that remained open were henceforth restricted to specific hours of the day and certain days of the week—

basically, closed whenever you needed them. A security man was stationed at the entrance, and cottagers required a plastic-coated identification card to get in.

(It struck me, as one who has worked as a journalist in Ottawa, that these were precisely the same rules for getting into the House of Commons. But I suppose garbage is garbage, no matter where it's found. The difference, however, between the dump on Muskoka Road 8 and Question Period is that there was always stuff of real value to be found in the dump.)

It will be properly broadcast that much was gained when the dumps were closed, but quietly said by some of us that something small was also lost. No longer would there be that mad, yelling rush to the truck when word travels among the children that a load of poplar branches is about to be hauled off to the dump. No longer would they return with distinctive smells in their hair and spent shotgun shells in their pockets.

No longer could they stomp about somehow missing the broken glass and jagged cans—and come back dragging such fabulous finds as snowmobile cowlings, broken steering wheels, mouse-infested cushions, dog-eared copies of the May 1962 *Reader's Digest,* three-legged chairs, torn screening, putty that has turned to stone—and a working electric kettle with nothing wrong with it but a frayed cord.

Gone forever those sweet July evenings when the car was filled with twice as many children as seatbelts, when the long, twisting run was made with the windows down and the summer air cupping in on our singing faces. Never again those spine-tingling moments when the headlights would be dashed as we turned off the main road and readied a flashlight so that once the engine was killed and pitch silence settled again over the dump, an old bear and her cubs might be caught ambling out of the woods for a late-night snack. No longer would we feel the thrill of winding down a window when a bear wandered close—the children screaming with the mad delight of knowing for certain there is indeed something out there. And old men with nothing but time on their hands—what of them? No longer can you pull into the dump and see an old pair of blue-veined, hairy legs in yellow shorts sticking out of a postwar Kelvinator.

I used to wonder what would happen if I drove into the dump with a bag of fresh fish guts and an old electric stove, threw them both out, hid behind the bushes, and waited. Who would strike first? A bear after the fish guts or an old man after a working element? Now I will never know.

I won't go into the irony of closing off these backroad delights to save the environment when recycling is supposed to be a big part of caring for this planet. What better example is there of inspired recycling than the summer dump? I know this is a foolish argument, and it is only mentioned in passing because, as is so often the case at a funeral, you don't know what to say about something you can do nothing about.

It is almost time to turn on the radio—yes, an old car radio from the dump. And then I will take out the cottage log book and read what was really special about the summers that are now a memory. We have been through the year of the snapping turtle. The year the big tree went down in the storm. The year of the big trout. Sometimes there is a dispute about the event that mattered most. But not that particular summer, not the year they closed the dumps.

Fishing

Decisions, decisions, decisions ...

The fish are calling. If you listen closely enough, you will hear the soft kiss of the lake trout as it rolls just beyond the shoal. Perhaps it is time to break out the steel line. Or perhaps this is the day to hike in to the secret lake and fly-fish from the hidden canoe. There are bass in the shallows, speckles in the creek, and lakers down so deep it is a wonder they have not frozen solid. I could chase them all—or I could just take a line and a hook and a worm, plastic if you insist, clip on a bobber, and toss the works off the end of the dock. And then go back to my book and coffee and hope nothing whatsoever happens.

It's still fishing.

It has been some time, centuries, in fact, since Lord Byron attacked this activity as "the stupidest of pretended sports," but the real stupidity belonged to the doomed poet, who didn't understand at all the quintessential fact of fishing: It is not a sport at all. Never has been, never should be.

I have fished all my life. My father fished all his, caught his last lake trout when he was well into his eighties, and wanted to stay out longer, even though the light was fast fading and nothing had hit for two hours. He was, by any measure, a Canadian eccentric, living so deep in the bush there was not even radio reception, yet surrounded by books that ranged from the latest Andy Capp collection to a dog-eared copy of Izaak Walton's *The Compleat Angler*. The full title of Walton's book, incidentally, was *The Contemplative Man's Recreation: Being a Discourse of Fish and Fishing, Not Unworthy the Perusal of Most Anglers*. It was first published in 1653 and, according to the *New York Times,* the only 350-year-old book that has been printed continually since its very first edition, with no revisions ever required.

I can understand why. "I have laid aside business," Izaak Walton wrote such a long time ago, "and gone a fishing." This deliberate disconnect with business my father understood. It was how he relaxed after long days at the mill. Once he finally retired and was able, for the first time in his life, to watch television, he could not believe that they had tried to turn fishing into programming. He would sit in front of the television and offer play-by-play commentary— "Tsk-tsk-tsk-tsk-tsk ..."—as silly men who couldn't decide whether they wanted to look like NASCAR racing drivers or U.S. Marine helicopter pilots flew around the lake on tangerine-flaked boats powered by 150-hp Mercs.

He counted himself a fisherman the equal of Simon the Apostle and Izaak Walton, but these shows made no more sense to him than Jerry Springer makes to happily married couples. Fishing, as he understood it, was about neither action nor explanation nor, for that matter, even conversation. My father never got to read David Adams Richards's lovely *Lines on the Water: A Fisherman's Life on the Miramichi*, but he didn't have to in order to agree with Richards's point that "There are a great many books that talk about the poetry of fishing, and yet silence might be the best way to understand it."

Silence isn't very conducive to television, but silence would certainly be a welcome visitor to those inane fishing shows that never seem to shut up about "structure" and what baits they're using and, of course, what sponsors are paying good dollars to hear their products mentioned. In attempting to make a "sport" out of something that is, at worst, a recreation and, at best, a way of life, these people have become their own parody. Size doesn't matter to true fishers any more than it does to true lovers.

Roderick Haig-Brown, the legendary West Coast fly-fisherman, eventually got to the point where he counted a day equally successful if he caught a nice king salmon or just happened to catch the light falling on the water in a certain way. "Perhaps," Haig-Brown mused in conclusion, "fishing is, for me, only an excuse to be near rivers."

I offer no preaching about fishing. Those who do not care for it sometimes ask me how I don't find it "boring," and I smile and say, "But that, you see, is precisely the point." I claim no expertise in fishing and couldn't care less about it. I am equally inept with fly, spinner, or steel line. My father had the soft, sure hands of a good fisher, and those hands clearly leaped a generation to his grandson and several granddaughters, but so what?

Let them tell their tales of great fish caught and lost. I alone own the story of bringing half a Cree village to its knees in tears of laughter when I cast a brand-new Lucky Strike lure off a dock one fine summer day in James Bay and had it wrap thirteen times around the neck of a wooden duck decoy some of the hunters had anchored off the end of the dock to bring in a wayward meal or two. I know it was thirteen times because one elderly woman loudly counted out in Cree as she and others watched two young boys paddle out and free the poor decoy from my precision cast.

Big deal. It doesn't bother me at all that others might find fishing meaningless and boring. Why, I ask, are these considered negatives? The great appeal of fly-fishing to the corporate and politically successful, both men and women, is that they are able to move out of range of cellphones and meetings and daily newspapers. The only deadlines are the rising and setting sun. It is the great nothing of it all that adds up to such a refreshing experience.

Stephen Leacock once wrote an essay called *Why Do We Fish?* and opened with the brilliant observation, "This article is intended to put the reader to sleep. Let it be understood right away that real fishermen don't go fishing for the sake of the fish. They pretend they do." Like Izaak Walton, Stephen Leacock stands the test of time. May neither of them ever go out of print.

I once asked my father what it was that he loved about trout fishing with steel line—the one fishing style where you cannot see what might be going on beneath the surface. "I like the suspense," he said. "The anticipation. You're up here. They're down there. Maybe they'll hit today. Maybe they won't."

It wouldn't work on a television show, but it works in real life. My father spent nearly ninety years fishing for trout and never seemed to much care if they were hitting or not. He liked the "act" of fishing: the preparation, the water, the loons, the first draw on an unfiltered Player's cigarette after the line has been let out and there is nothing to do but work the rod and wait. He always spit on his bait before dropping it over the side. "Why?" I often asked him. He didn't know. He just did it. He understood that nothing about fishing has to make sense. All you have to do is enjoy it.

Times have changed, of course. We no longer count on fish for food. With extremely rare exceptions, we and everyone else we know release everything that is caught. Our son, who makes his own flies, refuses to fish with barbed hooks.

It is not a pastime without criticism—there will, surely, one day be a significant fishes' rights movement—and it may even one day come to the point where it will be illegal to fish with worm or even hook. But the odd thing is, we'll still be out here, still "dropping a line," even if, in the end, that's all we're allowed to put in the water. The line connects us, whether or not there's a fish or even a hook on the other end, to something we seem to need in life. That line is a conductor, and it's not so much what it catches, but also what it releases.

Town Survival Manual

It has just occurred to me that there is a gaping hole in the cottage bookcase. It has nothing to do with the porcupine who sometimes crawls in under the deck and treats our cabin as if it were made of gingerbread; nothing to do with last June's end-of-school bash that we were specifically *not* invited to; nothing, even, to do with the guy down the bay who has, over the years, borrowed everything but the children. Those he could happily forget to return.

No, the gap has to do with missed opportunity. We have shelves of books on tripping and tracking, on bird, plant, and animal identification—everything you could ever need when it comes to survival in the deep, dark woods. There are pamphlets on how to identify poison ivy and dangerous mushrooms—even one on how to behave during bear attacks, the recommended course of action directly opposite for brown fur or black. Mercy on the colour blind. What is missing, it strikes me, is a handy *Survival Manual for Going to Town*.

We must first acknowledge that many cottagers are as drawn to town as surely as they are to the lake. The only explanation I have ever heard for this that makes sense is that butter tarts contain a hypnotic ingredient passed down through the generations to those who make a living off summer visitors.

Nothing else explains why normally sane people will voluntarily leave the hammock and head into town on dust-choked roads to spend an afternoon dragging themselves about store parking lots so hot the pavement has gone spongy. And nothing will ever explain why anyone would ever head for town on a summer day when the wind is out of the north, a cold rain is drumming on the cottage roof, and the line-up of cars carrying cottagers desperate for something to do runs for twenty blocks on both sides of the old swing bridge.

It is not hard to imagine some of the "survival" hints such a manual might contain:

- Only a fool would take back beer bottles on a Friday night or in any twenty-four-hour period preceding or following a holiday weekend.
- The last true bargain of any sort in cottage country was likely in 1868, when an Irishman named Paul Dane purchased Beaumaris Island in Lake Muskoka's Millionaire's Row for $101.

- The only place in the solar system hotter than the planet Jupiter at noon—430°C (810°F)—will be the front seat of the car you thought you'd parked in the shade.

- Seasoned town trekkers know better than to "browse" through the Canadian Tire tackle section. Reach out for a few twelve-inch leaders and soon you're standing in the cash line with a basket of lures, line, hooks, and aroma-enhanced baits worth more than the car in which you drove into town.

- The safest way to cross a street in cottage country is to step out and then wave graciously as the distracted drivers screech to a halt. Stoplights in summer towns mean different things: yellow means gun it; red means ignore it; and green means nothing, since no one can move in any direction anyway.

- It is a myth that you can get fit on frozen yogurt.

That there would be a market for such a manual is undeniable—and I intend to fill it. All I need is some paper to get started. And since I have to go to town anyway, I might as well pick up some butter tarts while I'm there.

July 13

S	M	T	W	T	F	S
				1	2	3
4	5	6	7	8	9	10
11	12	⑬	14	15	16	17
18	19	20	21	22	23	24
25	26	27	28	29	30	31

29° C. The hot spell continues. Up early and paddling around the far point in search of bass, but nothing hit. Saw the old snapping turtle on its favourite log—or, more accurately, I "heard" the turtle as it slipped off and splashed into the lake. It was still and clear, so I was able to follow a while in the canoe, watching as he or she twisted and turned among the stumps and rocks of the bay we call the "boneyard" because it is filled with so much sun-bleached driftwood.

The Snapping Turtle

It just may be that if their personality matched their looks, there would be no cottage country. They hold a special place in Canadian society. As instantly recognizable as the beaver, they have never become a symbol for anything but fear. They are found on no coin, no bill; and while other wildlife creatures like the bear become part of literature, they are stuck in folklore.

Children in other parts of the world might be unable to sleep for fear of snakes and monsters under the bed, but it is the children of cottage country who know a far greater terror is found lurking beneath the dock: the snapping turtle!

I am a turtle lover. I love to catch them sunning or watch them doing their slow-motion space walks along the rocks. Yet like most people, I, too, sometimes feel that primeval shudder when I stand at the edge of the dock about to dive, and see that large, dark shadow slip through a sunbeam and down into the stumps and deadheads. It may be irrational, but one startled blink seems capable of erasing a million years of evolution.

My experience with snapping turtles goes back to Lake of Two Rivers, where one self-assigned task of the old ranger was to keep the little ponds outside the Algonquin Park museum stocked with what was likely its major draw in the fifties and sixties: snappers with shells the size of car tires.

If a snapper were foolish enough to draw up on the rocks along our point to lie in the sun, the ranger would pull a heavy burlap sack out of the icehouse or the trunk of his old car, sometimes sneak up and tip the creature over with a rake or shovel, work it into the burlap, throw the sack over his back, and head off toward the museum. Sometimes the capture required several men and heavy rope, and while I never saw one of the men bitten, I do recall one turtle that, with a single chomp, splintered a rake handle in two. The snappers were never harmed. They were fed and stared at and photographed all summer and eventually let go to lie in the sun for another century or so.

There has never been a summer without a turtle story. My older brother, Jim, and I are still laughed at for the wonderful catch of speckles we foolishly tied to a stringer and left in shallow water to keep cool and fresh, only to return and find nothing left but the heads.

Our youngest daughter, Jocelyn, isn't allowed to forget the day she thought she'd caught a world-record bass off the dock, only to find herself in a tug of war with a snapper that probably outweighed her. And no one will ever forget the time little Hope, from up the lake, went sailing out on the end of the rope and, just as she was about to drop, looked down into those beady eyes that always lead to that familiar spine-chilling call:

"TURRRRRRRTTLLLLLE!"

At one point, to appease nervous children, I used to chase the snappers down with large fish nets, cart them up the hill, drive off to the nearest non-peopled water, and let them go. I have no idea whether all big turtles just look the same or if, in fact, they do work their way back, but I eventually gave up on such foolishness.

I then tried education. I gathered together all the available material and explained that, in over five hundred years of Canadian skinny-dipping, no one has ever lost an appendage to a snapping turtle. In water, snappers are precisely as they appear to be: calm, gracious, and shy, with no interest in confrontation. Out of water, they are to be left alone. Period.

Youngest daughter Jocelyn, however, could not shake the fear that had grown out of that much-earlier tug of war with the one we came to call "Snappy." If a turtle was sighted, the water was emptied. This went on summer after summer until, one lovely July day, she was in the boat watching a loon family dive and fish in the near bay. Suddenly the baby disappeared as a large shadow passed beneath it. The snapper had struck.

Jocelyn never stopped to think. She chased down the turtle escaping with the little loon in its mouth, reached down and hauled the big snapping turtle out by the edge of the shell, and, holding it like a serving tray, shook it for all she was worth before dropping turtle and loon back into the lake. When the turtle surfaced, its mouth was empty and the baby loon freed.

Career tug of war stats: Snappy I, Jocelyn I. The irrational fear was gone, forever.

Leaving only the bears along the outhouse path to be dealt with at a later date.

The Art of Puttering

Forty years later, I still maintain it was an accident.

I had never before even seen cherry tomatoes. I had, admittedly, spent time at the Lake Joseph cottage of my great high-school friend, Ralph, now my brother-in-law, but the Coxes were recently transplanted city people, far more sophisticated than this particular country bumpkin, and I had no idea whatsoever how to eat one of those tiny, shining orange-red balls I found on the side of my sandwich plate that warm August afternoon on Lake Joe.

I held one of them up between thumb and forefinger, opened my mouth, and, I thought very smartly, bit down with my front teeth in order to halve it—only to have the miniature tomato explode straight across the table and into the face of my friend's father.

Some thought it deliberate, an act of revenge. It had, after all, been a difficult day being around Ed Cox, chief project director of a small bay at the north end of the big lake. We had spent most of the day jacking up and balancing the cottage, shingling the roof of a sleeping cabin, hauling and spreading a load of dirt on the horseshoe pit, and raking the beach area for loose stones and water weeds.

Someone—guess who?—had then foolishly left the rake lying on the dock, teeth up, a cartoon accident waiting to happen, until Ed Cox, missing only the white foreman's helmet, happened to survey the project area and discover that one of the workers had slacked off just enough to endanger the entire populace of cottage country. "What kind of an *idiot* would leave a rake sitting around like that?" is, I believe, roughly the way he worded it.

Put that incident together with the attack of the killer cherry tomato and you can understand how events came to be misinterpreted. The truth is, I deeply liked Ed Cox. He was generous, usually good-humoured, and allowed visiting teenagers to drive the ski boat. But he was also a putterer—the greatest putterer I have ever known, in fact, and in this we distinctly parted company. Ed Cox was never so happy as when he was in his perfectly organized workshed, whistling a Perry Como song as he sharpened a small scythe or searched for a nut and washer to fit a found bolt. He kept lists—made lists of his lists for all I know—and spent his few idle moments with a steaming cup of coffee and a pencil, ticking off what had been done and what still had to be done, and scribbling out projects for tomorrow and the next day and possibly even the next ten summers.

I am the opposite of the projects person. If I kept a cottage list of "must" things to do, it would read something like this:

- Have breakfast on the deck.
- Paddle before the wind comes up.
- Have second cup of coffee.
- Boat 'round lake looking for people to bug.
- Fish.
- Join kids in swinging off rope.
- Eat lunch.
- Start new mystery novel.
- Nap.
- Hike into bush with dog.
- Think about having cold beer before dinner.
- Eat on deck.
- Paddle or visit around lake.
- Build campfire.

I married a project manager. Ellen is one of those who must have something concrete (sometimes literally) to do at the cottage or else there is no point in being there. I, of course, would argue that the point *is* to do nothing. Fortunately, it works for us. She builds the steps, replaces the deck, puts up the shed, hammers together the docks, puts in the new steps, and has backpocket plans for everything from a refurbished outhouse to a new bunkie somewhere down the road. I did once install a small electric heater one winter weekend. It had to be plugged in. So I am not entirely useless.

This profound difference in cottage personalities has long fascinated me. Ellen's father, Lloyd, was much like Ed Cox, so project-oriented that the cottage became more vocation than vacation, with pure, and obvious, pleasure coming from mapping out a plan and executing it—even if it meant extra trips to town for $1\frac{1}{4}$-inch nails or a fresh pack of putty or whatever might be needed for what would never, in a dozen summers, even occur to me to do.

Perhaps it is an inherited trait. My own father never took a holiday in the Ontario bush for the very good reason that he was already in the bush and didn't bother with holidays. He was a logger who spent what little spare time he had reading and fishing and rooting around in a small cold creek for the beer he'd hidden there. The only thing I've changed is that we have a refrigerator.

He had lost his father when he was only four years old and once explained to me that he had no tools and no knowledge of how to use them because he had no one to pass the knowledge down to him, and thus could pass nothing down to me. My own son adores tools—he borrows his mother's.

I will sometimes be found scanning one of the cabin's old 1960s issues of *Popular Mechanics,* but it is not in search of old projects to make new. It is, instead, to wonder where the hell my household robot is that was supposed to be doing all that sort of work by the year 2000.

I have no idea the image this projects around the lake, but I accept that it is not a good one. *"MacGregor"*—I can almost hear the gossip drifting across the bay on a clear night—*"Isn't he the one who can spend an entire day looking for the perfect tree fungus for the kids to draw on?"*

Newspapers publish endless articles about the importance of balancing work with leisure, but I have long mastered this skill without the slightest instruction:

- Plug in the toaster, go for a canoe ride.
- Pound a nail into the tree to hold the swim goggles, go for a long bike ride.
- Look up the telephone number of a good handyman, go fishing.

I do, however, have one project still to consider, one that, at the moment, sits at the very top of my list of "Things to Do Before This Summer Is Out": Close mouth on cherry tomatoes before biting down.

The Fish Finder

I have two recurring dreams. One is a nightmare from which I cannot wake fast enough. In it, I have just been told I must go back and repeat grade twelve. "But I *already* repeated it," I plead, but to no avail. A mistake has been found in the Huntsville High School records and now I must return, for a third time, to the torture chambers of chemistry and algebra. The other is a dream I embrace like an old friend. The water has all drained out of the lake. The lake bottom is wet and muddy, but still firm enough that I can race across it, checking out the shoals and scooping up lost lures.

I have a thing about knowing what lies beneath the surface. When I was young and still at Lake of Two Rivers, I would lie on the high rocks and watch bass lolling in the early morning sun. Now, on another lake on the edge of Algonquin Park, I cannot resist those mornings when the lake becomes a pane of glass, as I paddle the shoreline in search of minnows and, with luck, a swimming turtle.

Water, Thoreau believed, "is earth's eye; looking into which the beholder measures the depth of his own nature." If this is so, then I am a shallow person. I stare down, endlessly, at what I can see of a lake bottom, which restricts me to calm, sunny days. I will look at anything, even stumps. I count it a highlight of my life that I was in a canoe, with two of the kids, when a loon dove under us and let loose what we have always presumed bears do in the woods. Just for the record, it is like a blast of white shrapnel.

My interest in the secrets of the lake bottom is the reason I became the only person ever known to paddle about with a fish finder but no fishing pole. I picked up the fish finder during one Stanley Cup playoff series, and I remember standing in a Dallas store staring at the demonstration and thinking that for $79.99 American—then roughly the equivalent of $1.2 million Canadian—I could finally find out how far the shoal in the middle of the lake runs.

The fish finder would make up for my bad hands. My father had "soft hands" for fishing, but they somehow skipped a generation and ended up with my son. With nothing more than a trolling rod, these hands can *feel out* a lake, bouncing a lure off the bottom until a perfect map forms in their memory. I do not have that ability. I do, however, have a plastic credit card that provided me with the electronic equivalent.

The day I set out to map the bottom two lake friends, John and Denis, decided to come along for the ride—and presumably to find out where the lunkers are hiding. I attached the suction cup, clicked the "on" button, and we set out to map the last great unexplored mystery of the world. The little machine beeped a few times, and something dark began rolling across the graph, complete with readout numbers. I was, finally, *seeing* bottom.

"It's 120 feet deep here!" I called out. I could barely believe it. I would have guessed sixty, at best.

"Twenty feet now!" Denis called out.

We leaned over the sides, expecting to see a small volcano rising where previously we had thought there might be a shoal.

"Look at the fish!" John yelled.

We stared, stunned: the graph was filling with fish after fish after fish, the beeping growing louder and louder. Finally, a beep like an alarm signal.

"Good God!" I cried, pointing. "There's a *whale* down there!"

Whatever it was lurking beneath the deep, it took up the whole width of the graph. Smaller fish seemed to scatter. The beeper was sounding as if one of us had just walked through an airport check wearing a nail apron.

Denis shook his head: "Impossible." He reached out and slowly ran a calloused finger—he's handy, I am not—down the side of the fish finder until he found a small switch, which he pushed. Suddenly the screen changed: seventy feet deep, no fish.

I looked at it, thinking he had broken my Texas prize. "What happened?"

He looked up, smiling in pity. "You forgot to switch it over from 'demonstration' mode."

I sat there, blinking in the morning sun, knowing it was only a matter of hours before night fell and, once again, I would be headed back to grade twelve.

July 23

S	M	T	W	T	F	S
				~~1~~	~~2~~	~~3~~
~~4~~	~~5~~	~~6~~	~~7~~	~~8~~	~~9~~	~~10~~
~~11~~	~~12~~	~~13~~	~~14~~	~~15~~	~~16~~	~~17~~
~~18~~	~~19~~	~~20~~	~~21~~	~~22~~	(23)	24
25	26	27	28	29	30	31

23°C and lovely. But we have to leave! Just the two of us, and the dog. We are being booted out, an increasingly common phenomenon in recent years. "Friends are coming up" … "It's going to be a party" … "You won't want to be there" … True enough, we don't—but this isn't quite the way we imagined matters when they were still playing with toads in the old washtub and I was the one drinking beer on the deck, is it?

Kicked Out

We are heading up Highway 11 north, just beginning the climb before the long drop into Sundridge, heading fast for North Bay and sanctuary. Up ahead, up through the rain and smeared flies of this stone-pocked windshield, there will be blood relations glad to see me, insisting that I stay, delighted with my wit, my charm, my deep, abiding sense of sharing.

This, at least, is some comfort as I drive, hunched down over the steering wheel, unable yet to look at the rear-view mirror that is unfolding so quickly with hardwood bush and water where I am no longer welcome. I also do not look up for fear of catching a glimpse of myself—middle-aged and crazy, the hypocrite of the millennium.

Perhaps I should explain myself. Two-and-a-half hours earlier, Ellen, the dog Bandit, and I were all standing at the end of the dock, thinking about what we might do once the rain had completely let up. There was a slight breeze in the air—perfect for sailing. The water was mid-July warm—perfect for swimming. There was cold beer in the fridge, an untouched mystery novel, an unfilled hammock perfect for me.

Because we believe where we stood to be the most beautiful spot on earth, we had the world at our command. A day beginning to bake; a memory beginning to rise. And yet, almost as soon as I turned to climb the hill to answer the call of the cottage beer—a high-pitched tone dogs can't hear but certain neighbours always seem to—an older daughter was standing on the plank heading out onto the dock.

Christine was at this moment nineteen years old—an age I am forced to revisit as I drive through Sundridge headed for South River—and healthy, beautiful, and, I had believed right up until that moment, well adjusted. Her big brown eyes were pleading, her face caught in that open-mouthed moment between hope and frustration. "You *are* leaving, *aren't* you?" she asked. Thunder roared over the pines. Lightning sheared the plank that connected parent and child. The 1960s smashed head-on into the next century. I smiled. A '60s smile that said everything is cool, relax, do your own thing, nobody gets hurt. "You *really* want us to?"

The eyes spoke, flash lightning behind long lashes: *What-the-hell-do-you-think?*

"Okay," I said, lip trembling. "We're outta here."

And an hour later, we were, as per our agreement. It had never been written down, never notarized, but it had been spoken several times during the winter months, when there always seems a large enough gap between fantasy and reality that it will never actually come to this. Both older daughters had often asked if, at some time, they and their friends could go, alone, up to the cottage for a weekend.

This, after all, is what we say cottages are all about: genetic roots and rocks. Cottages, we are told by bankers and accountants and our own deepening sense of mortality, are made for passing on.

But do we really need to practise?

On through South River and toward Trout Creek I drive, up toward Powassan and Callander and onto the four lanes again, where the division between coming and going is not only wider, but permanent. I still have not looked back. I do not need to. The imagination can see everything that has been left behind: the shear pin gone on the propeller, a tipped canoe, an axe through a foot, broken beer bottles around the barbecue, a campfire that gets away, the cottage burned to the ground, police surrounding the lot, illegitimate children hopping about the grass like a hatch of spring toads …

Give your head a shake!

I fret because I know. I worry because I am no fool, no matter what this sounds like so far. I know what it is to be young and at a cottage, alone. No parents, no neighbours, no police, no rules, no bedtime, no common sense. I grew up in cottage country; a teenager with all of north

Muskoka at the doorstep, the sacred rites of passage nothing more than a quick stop at the beer store with an older acquaintance willing to buy for you, a friend with a car for the weekend, a turn off the main highway onto a secondary road, a turn off the secondary road to a cottage road, and a key. A key meant we were among the more responsible local teenagers.

Because I also grew up at cottages, I have often talked to our children about the "cottage" experience and what it can mean for a lifetime. I have told them about deer and bears, about mink that would steal your trout before you could clean them, and I have shown them how to pick up crawfish and take off bloodsuckers, and taught them how to split kindling and build fires and even play, and enjoy, Snakes and Ladders. But eventually they come to realize that this cannot be all we did at cottages. If a cottage is about genetics, then it must also be about hormones. Yet while we speak so glowingly of one, we say nothing of the other.

They do not know that their father once, literally, hung from the rafters of a friend's cottage up by Lake Bernard. They do not know of the time we wired speakers into the trees over on Lake Joseph and played Jimi Hendrix and Janis Joplin all one balmy fall night. They do not know about the under-aged drinking and under-aged driving and the poker and the cigars and the yelling and screaming into the night. And, thank God, they do not know what it is like to stick one's head halfway down a cottage outhouse and pay the price of being young and immature and foolish and, well, *Canadian*. At least I hope not. I pray not.

As I have been researching this phenomenon for most of my life, it should hardly surprise me when hormones kick in on our own children. After all, I was once a teenager in cottage country, and it is a well-known, scientific fact that the teenage male brain cannot look even at rolling clouds without seeing heaving breasts.

Summer in cottage country has always had a teenage madness to it that exceeds even the normal hormonal ravings of the rest of the year. I cannot speak for those city kids who headed north each summer, but I can speak for the locals who had their own peculiar approach to the coming of summer and, more significantly, the arrival of the cottagers and campers. In our town, "going steady" meant September to late spring. Around the time cottagers were opening up, we began breaking up. Just like the ice in the bay.

It was almost an unspoken agreement in these summer towns that solid relationships closed down for the season. Convenient fights would be picked, awkward phone calls placed or never returned: whatever it took to shake off the known relationship for the imaginary ones—the blonde sunbather, the passing canoes filled with randy campers ...

This bizarre Frankie-and-Annette lifestyle change had both advantages and disadvantages, of course. A seventeen-year-old male is not going to complain when his town's romance pool of, say, five hundred bodies in winter swells to 50,000—none of them bundled up in heavy clothing. On the other hand, when you count yourself lucky to borrow the old man's half-ton for a Saturday night, it's difficult to compete with a Corvette or a gleaming runabout.

But no matter whether you arrive by Corvette or were already there by circumstance, summer romance is a precious, humorous rite of passage. For summer is the time when Canadian teenagers come as close as humans ever do to experiencing life as insects. When the hatch is upon us—pick any long weekend—they flare like the mayfly, bursting over the water in blinding droves, soaring magnificently in the celebration of their brief, frantic mating period. In the Canadian summer, the teenagers of cottage country lead lives—often *several* lives—of loud desperation.

Given that understanding, then, should I not have been grateful that our second daughter had merely asked if she and her special friend could have some quiet time alone? Why should they not? Both are beyond the age of major-ity. They are so responsible in all other walks of their lives that, at times, I wonder if *I* were adopted. They go to school, work hard at their jobs, and have surely been looking forward to this weekend break for some time, never once imagining themselves hanging around with a bunch of younger kids and a couple of dull adults, one of whom they claim—incorrectly, I should point out—is beginning to wear his jogging pants too high.

But I also know a secret—and that is that we, too, were responsible. Deceptively responsible. How many times did we combine a case of twenty-four with putting in a dock? We hooked up the water, cleaned out the mouse droppings, took apart chimney pipes, aired out rugs, jacked up sleeping cabins, hammered on shingles, split wood, and hauled rocks for new piers. And then we partied. We did this because just as the price of youth is excess, the price of a cottage was invariably laid out in specific instructions from parents who—bizarre and impossible as this sounds—probably were just about the same age as I am this day heading into North Bay.

Perhaps they thought if they kept us busy they would keep us out of trouble. How little they knew that a dock, for example, can be put in and levelled perfectly in less than thirty minutes if the water temperature is roughly two degrees above freezing and there is a case of beer waiting on the stoop. We weren't stupid. But, then again, maybe neither were they.

That teenage sense of responsibility seemed to flow out of two different sources. The first, obviously, was that everyone understood that this was the price of admission, and that no one was ever going to be invited back if they screwed up. The second, and perhaps most powerful, came naturally to whichever youngster had the direct family ties to whatever place you were about to invade. This went beyond the price of admission. It went beyond, perhaps, even fear of the parents' surprise arrival. (*We started out for a nice drive, and somehow ended up here.*) No, it had something to do, I suspect, with waking up the next morning and realizing that you and your friends have just desecrated the family place of worship. It left you with two choices: one, spend the rest of the weekend cleaning up, or two—and I like to think the one more often chosen—take care as you go, and treat the place as if parents or grandparents were there with you. Even though—*ha ha, ho ho, hee hee*—they most certainly, and happily, are not.

Our hope was always that our children, soon to number four, would want to bring their friends up to the cottage. Soon enough, it seemed, they *wouldn't* come unless they could bring a friend. Not all experiences were good—we remember the kid who hid under a sheet most of the weekend in a back bedroom and the boyfriend who survived four days without once trying the outhouse—but most were marvellous. We all enjoyed them and, somewhat naively, came to expect that cottage life would go on as real life refuses to: in a state of blissful suspension, the sun always shining, the water warm, the kids forever young and squealing, the parents all knowing, all involved, always welcome.

The eldest of the four is now, I almost regret to say, a young woman flourishing on her own in the city. As Kerry was the first to bring a friend, the first to bring a boyfriend—and, it seems naturally to follow, first to give us the boot—I am obliged to turn to her for the other side of this perplexing situation. Instead of dwelling on what can go wrong, she advises, think about what can go right. "The fun about having a cottage all to yourself" she tells me in a note I will now try to memorize, "is that you can show your friends what you want them to know about your past and your family—i.e., where you used to spit watermelon seeds, the sand pit—and shield them from the more embarrassing parts like the Barbie pond where we used to play dolls, or the picture of me foaming marshmallows at the mouth. What do you do when the parents are away? Talk about your family, your identity, your experiences. You just need time to work out your little scenes of building a reputation for yourself without the help of dirty-diaper stories."

That, of course, hurts. I tell those diaper stories so well, after all.

"Being at the cottage without parents," she writes, "is kind of like playing house, but in a more far-out, down-to-earth, fun-in-the-sun way. It's the first vacation I ever went on without my parents. It was relaxing, but safe—

because I'd been going there all my life. It was the best place to try out friends, too. You always have the upper hand because you know the place better, and if you ever lose the reflection of who you really are, under all that pretending and searching, all you have to do is look off the end of the dock."

All you have to do is look off the end of the dock. I think about that through the long day and night the dog, Ellen, and I spend at the North Bay lake where we are not only made welcome but bade stay. I, of course, find a million reasons for racing back at the earliest opportunity: ... *promised the neighbour I'd help him fell a tree ... have to complain about the property taxes ... think I left the fridge open ... the radio said something about tornadoes ...*

We drive back down Highway 11 at twice the speed we came up. Powassan, Trout Creek, South River, Sundridge, Burk's Falls, Novar—they slip by so fast the rear-view mirror doesn't even catch them as they pass. Left on to Highway 60, fishtail up Muskoka Road 8, turn at the government dock, and bottom out twice on the rough road past the hydro line. Coke spills, the dog yelps—but we are back home, and in full investigative mode.

They are sunning on the deck. They have been swimming. The boat has been cleaned out and docked with proper knots. The place has been vacuumed. A fresh salad is in the refrigerator. Wood has been chopped and piled in that mysterious, perfect, building-block style that I have never been able to master. My beer is cold and waiting.

"Did you have a good time?" she asks.

"Yeah, sure—*you*?"

"Nice," she says. "So relaxing. We did some work."

I nod, biting my lip. Is this the time to play my trump card? Do I let her know that I know why, too? *You did some work because only a few hours ago there was a motorcycle gang living here, wasn't there?* But I say nothing. The younger kids are going swimming and, bless their mature little hearts, have asked me to join them. The dog barks happily, jumping at me. She, at least, has never asked to bring a friend. She, it goes without saying, has never asked for a weekend here alone.

I stand at the edge of the dock and note that the lake is still there. The boat runs. The only smell of fire is the neighbour's barbecue. The canoe is turned over, the paddles put away. That sound in the distance is a loon, not a police siren.

For a moment I remember something the second-oldest said to us last summer. She had not wanted to go to the cottage. She had said, in a moment she may well forget now, that the cottage was *our* big deal, not hers, and that it really meant nothing to her. It stung to hear her say that. But now, less than a year later, she is back at the cottage. Sharing it with a friend. Probably boasting about those wonderful, treasured, irreplaceable times we have all had here together. Perhaps she has even told some of my stories.

But she is back—and that is what matters—she is back because there is something about this place she wants for her own. She may even have her own stories now. Not that I am old enough yet to hear them.

July 25

S M T W T F S
~~1~~ ~~2~~ ~~3~~
~~4~~ ~~5~~ ~~6~~ ~~7~~ ~~8~~ ~~9~~ ~~10~~
~~11~~ ~~12~~ ~~13~~ ~~14~~ ~~15~~ ~~16~~ ~~17~~
~~18~~ ~~19~~ ~~20~~ ~~21~~ ~~22~~ ~~23~~ ~~24~~
(25) 26 27 28 29 30 31

27° C. Somewhat cloudy, light wind out of east. First knock on the head of this year—I was crawling under the deck in search of a dropped fork and the usual happened. I think I need stitches. The kids think it's the funniest thing that's happened all summer.

The Head Injury

It is a shame, really, that there isn't a field guide for some of the more exotic creatures of cottage country. Some are simple to identify: the first-timer couple and the too-clean Tilley hat; the hopelessly lost-in-timer with no socks for his loafers; the aging beer drinker who really shouldn't have ripped the sleeves off that T-shirt ... and, of course, the bald guy with the cut on his head.

I can think of no creature more closely identified with the lake than the bald guy with the big welt, the fresh cut, the bandage, or the scab on the top of his head. If we happen to see him in the city during the summer months, we automatically presume he has merely migrated south for the workweek and that sometime during the weekend past he must have been crawling under the cottage to check the water supply.

I knock my own head every summer, the scars a sort of phrenological journal of where I went wrong. Last year it was nothing other than searching for a magazine—unfortunately, not a *Cottage Life* feature on emergency first-aid when alone—and all I did was move one of the kids' beds out of the way so I could get closer to the closet shelf where the magazines are piled. I shoved the bed without remembering that, tucked between the headboard and the wall, we had stacked an older bed frame—causing one of the side supports to come falling down just as I reached to pick through the stack of magazines.

I don't know how long I lay there. I do know that there was a great amount of blood when I got up, and I wasn't sure, in fact, whether I was at the cottage or was lost with *Beagle 2* somewhere in a Mars crater.

For a long time I believed that the baseball cap was in part to blame for so many knocks to the summer skull. Bald and balding men wear baseball caps the way small children wear diapers—out of sheer necessity—and through experience I had become convinced that the cap brims were cutting off upper peripheral vision and were therefore as great a danger to their wearer as the noon sun they were trying to keep off. This notion was tossed out later in the summer when my older brother was visiting and, having finished his meal with his cap off, stood up too quickly and cranked his 6'1" into a cheap chandelier that would, in any profession-ally built cottage, have been hanging over the *centre* of the table, not so far *off centre* that it would become a menace.

One friend is convinced that hair also acts as antennae. A full head of hair, she says, may not only be a good buffer but an early-warning system for falling boards and too-close joists.

Daughter Jocelyn, who has hair as thick as a bunkie mattress and has never learned the art of mincing her words, has recommended that, this year, I take a simple initiative that will guarantee there will be no further scarring of the family brain trust.

"Take your hockey helmet to the cottage," she says. "And when you're there alone—wear it."

Sounds

We might have called it a pilgrimage, except the word seems much too large and presumes that others might care, when in fact it was only us: my cousin, Don McCormick; my mother, Helen; and me. An older woman—she would never agree to "elderly"—who had been born in the heart of Algonquin Park more than eighty years ago, and two middle-aged men who had both been born near the East Gate and raised not far from the West Gate.

Just us: three whose lives have always revolved around the Park and who had come again this July day to think of two recently lost connections—the older woman's husband and her daughter (my father and sister)—and to visit, once again, a rocky point where the wind is always in the pines and the lake soft and slapping under a granite overhang.

We had come here to listen to the past, the summer song of our collective lives. Some say that taste is the most accurate memory and sight the most immediate, but both had long vacated this familiar point on the north shore of Lake of Two Rivers.

Those late-July blueberries are small and bitter, unsuitable for pies. The log home is gone, along with the cabins, the floating dock, and the ice house. There is no longer a trail in from Highway 60; instead, one man in his forties and another in his fifties had to hack and push a path through so the one in her eighties, laughing as she tripped on rotted branches and slipped on club moss—we always called it princess pine—could get in here another time. God willing, not for the last.

There is nothing to see now but the broken-down fireplace and the stones that once held the flagpole. But it hardly matters: We sit and we can hear the snap of burning spruce, and the different snap a flag—a Union Jack—makes in a wind that is forever out of the west.

We cannot enter a log home that is no longer standing, but we enter, easily and happily, the sounds that stand guard for us, waiting: the wind and the water, the sound of this lake on this point—a voice that belongs nowhere else. We do not talk because there is nothing on anyone's mind that is not on the others' minds.

My mother sits on a large stone and watches Don and I dive from the high rocks much as we dove in the '50s and '60s, the splash the same, the whoop the same, the footholds getting back out the same, only slippery from disuse.

I wander off and find, back of where the outhouse once stood, a rusted old straight pipe that once carried the exhaust from our coal-oil-driven washing machine out the porch door. I cart it back and we stand and marvel at it, each hearing again the heavy burp of the machine in full throttle, the memory bittersweet in that it speaks to us of summers lost, but reminds, as well, of the rule that forbade swimming when the washing machine was on because no one, we were told, would ever hear our cries for help if we got in trouble.

We sit and eat and remember the sounds: the Scot at the end of the lake who would sometimes play the bagpipes under a full moon, the sound of the Evinrude 3 hp at the end of an evening troll when it would move flat out toward the dock—a red wooden boat that looked and sounded like it was hurrying but never seemed to come closer—and we would run to see if there were any fat lake trout for the next day's meal.

We hear again the creaking sound of the hand pump as the old park ranger, khaki shirt drenched black under the armpits, pushed enough water up the hill for a bath; the sound tongs make when they catch on a big square of ice; the squeak of the old roller as the fishing boat is hauled up onto the dock and out of the wind; the slam of the screen door.

The slam of the screen door. I can hear it, perfectly, if I shut my eyes. I can hear it if I open them. When I cannot hear it is when I look for it. A thousand screen doors have slammed since, but never, ever, one that had precisely the sound of the kitchen cabin door at Lake of Two Rivers. It sounded like dinner, like the hiss of a kerosene lamp, like a damp washcloth going over oilcloth, like an iron heating and spitting on the woodstove, like Pick-Up-Sticks dropping and the evening games under way.

My mother is into her eighties this day, and sometimes her voice cracks and catches, but we wonder if she called us in now as we take those last few dives from the high rocks if we would hit the water and be cleansed of the last forty years.

Sitting here on this rocky point in what some would foolishly call silence, I wonder what sounds from our own little cabin on a smaller lake will stay with our own children, the grandchildren of this older woman who taught us all to love the bush above all else.

There is, alas, no screen door that slams with the sweet certainty of the one now lost at Lake of Two Rivers. A metal storm door is hardly the same. But there are different sounds, and they speak to us of their own wonderful summers in their own mysterious ways.

The sounds of work: of a chainsaw starting up far too early in the day, of lumber being dropped at the government dock, of an outboard straining as a makeshift barge takes a septic tank and piles of new roof shingles down the lake. The different sound that comes from the same axe as it first chops too-green maple into firewood, then as it splits dry cedar into kindling. The whine of a circular saw, the sureness of a handsaw, the hollow, insistent knock of a hammer on nails.

The sounds of play: children on a diving dock, conversations drifting too loudly over a trolling motor, quiet library whispers from a canoe, the shouts and screams of water-skiers and tubers and knee-boarders and wakeboarders and whatever in God's name they have come up with this year to add another $500 to the Visa card.

The bad music of a cottage-country radio station and how the weather reports are always turned up too late. The knock a paddle makes on a gunwale when the "J" stroke is neither used nor understood. The magnificent, certain sound an expert canoeist will make—only in early morning or early evening—as he or she moves silently along the shore, the paddle in the water like the licking of lips. The futile roll and burble of a pedal boat being pedalled too quickly. The obnoxious, challenging roar of a personal watercraft, the one sound of summer that separates cottagers the way the American Civil War once split families.

Here on this rocky point where the three pilgrims have come to sit and listen, they remember the way rain fell here like it fell no other place on earth: thunder rumbling in the distance, then suddenly shattering overhead, the sizzle that lightning makes when it's much too close, hard rain

sweeping in curtains across the lake, a light rain ringing—
ringing!—on a still lake surface as we sat in the kitchen cabin,
the windows open, and stared into water virtually within
reach, and the sweetest sound of all—a soft rain on a sleeping-
cabin roof when there is neither ceiling nor leaks.

Sounds, too, are seasonal. In May, when we burst on the
lake like a human spring runoff, a ruffed grouse will begin
its drumming. At night, there are spring peepers. In July,
there is always a bullfrog. Sometimes, on a moonlit
summer's night, we hear wolves howling in the distance. In
August, when the sun is directly overhead, the cicadas will
start their buzz, and if anyone ever wondered if sound can
carry heat, they have not heard the cicada.

The sweetest sounds, of course, come from the birds—
even the grumpy croak of the great blue heron as it protests
every boat and canoe and walker that comes along and
sends it flying, in silly sequence, on and on and on along
the shoreline. The most memorable, of course, are the
various calls of the loon, a magnificent, complicated
language only longtime cottagers eventually come to
understand. But there are also the red-winged blackbirds
in the meadows and the white-throated sparrows in the
high trees. There is no sound more amusing than that
which trails a family of more than a dozen mergansers as
they follow one another over logs and rocks and lose a
trailer and circle back to start again. And no sound more

thrilling than the piercing shriek of an osprey diving for trout.

There are also the sounds we hate. The mosquitoes that have somehow made it in at night, their building whine the scream of the victorious. The sound of missed slaps. The heavier slap and shout of triumph that follows the death of a dreaded horsefly. The sounds that make us cringe in fall: the faraway, muffled burst of a shotgun, the crack of a rifle, the next sound a little closer, the next one too close.

In winter, there is a secret known only to those who have trekked in to cottages on isolated lakes and spent hours shivering beside a fireplace. Once the work has been done, if you stand outside on a still night there is no sound at all unless a tree happens to crack.

Nothing.

Nothing. The loudest sound of all. But not the most moving. Here on this rocky point on Lake of Two Rivers, it is the sound of the wind in the pines for us, just as it will be other special sounds for others. We sit and listen and the history of our family is in the pines: the old ranger and his wife, the long years my mother spent here as a young woman, the sound of the whistle at the mill that once stood across the lake and where the man who would become her husband worked, the babies she brought here, the large, extended family who counted this among the precious spots on earth.

And now, somehow, precious beyond even that. The old ranger and his wife, a husband who reached his eighties, a daughter just turned fifty—they are missing, time stunning us all with its brevity. And yet they are not gone. Not from here. Not from where the wind is always blowing, and where the sound in the pines says that we are all here, forever.

Gold Fever

They gathered Saturday night in a rustic camp hall, the speakers pausing each time the screen door announced a new arrival. They had come, the sixty or more summer cottagers, to find out what was going on.

"Are we all going to be rich—or what?" a young man with a raspy voice demanded of the mayor. It was an unusual question for a cottagers' association that traditionally has been more concerned with washboard roads, but then, this has hardly been a normal summer for this particular area.

I hesitate to locate this story any more clearly than to say the area borders Algonquin Park, for we are talking here of a matter that drives people mad: *gold fever*. The story begins harmlessly enough fifty years earlier, with a fisherman giving up and finding a "rusty" stone caught on his anchor. Struck by its peculiar beauty, he took it home with him, where it sat for years on the end of a mantle, until a visitor happened to suggest that he have it assayed. It turned out, the story goes, to be packed with gold and silver.

The cottagers began to wonder last fall when they discovered that most of the western side of the Park had been staked out. And over the winter, when a group called Canadian Gold Resources Inc. began hauling drilling apparatus out onto the ice, a full panic set in. Some cottagers wanted to know what this would do to their environment. Others wondered what it would mean to their pocketbooks. By summer, families who once moved about the rocks looking for raspberries now moved about the raspberries looking for rocks. And those who laughed at first soon grew as mad as the rest.

I was sitting on a government dock when a [then] ten-year-old let out a shout filled with both terror and hope, one that could be appreciated only after I had pulled forty-one small bloodsuckers off her feet and stared at what she carried in her hands: a small, egg-shaped rock that sparked in the sun like the cap in a millionaire's mouth. *Gold!* Naturally, being a mature, sensible parent, I indulged her fantasies. At night she would sit cradling the stone and dreaming of engines for wooden cars and farms, and she would ask: "Do you think it's really gold?"

"Perhaps."

"Who could tell me?"

"I don't know. A jeweller might know."

"I think," she said, "after I've found a million dollars worth I'll give the rest of it to poor people."

That seemed rather thoughtful, and once she had gone to sleep, I began to think of just what a gold strike could do for a very specific poor person. With a loon providing the background for my reveries, I paid off the mortgage, traded in the wreck, cleared up the Visa, and spent the March Break in Barbados. By morning I looked like Humphrey Bogart in *The Treasure of Sierra Madre:* unshaven, shifty-eyed, frothing.

"We're going in to town," I announced.

"What for?"

"The jeweller's."

An hour later we stood at the front door of Mr. Henry's jewellery store.

"Maybe it would be better not to find out," my daughter suggested. "That way, as long as he doesn't say it isn't gold, we can always hope." She did not understand that we had gone beyond hoping. We were now *banking* on it.

Mr. Henry stared patiently over his half-glasses, glancing down at the stone as if he had been doing it all summer.

"I'm afraid you've found pyrite," he said. "*Fool's* gold."

Later, at the meeting of concerned cottagers, the mayor shrugged his shoulders at the young man's question and turned to a councillor for help. Nothing more had been heard from Canadian Gold Resources Inc., the elderly councillor reported. "They packed up their bags and left— so you figure it out from there."

Everyone laughed, as if they had known all along. Yet when the meeting broke up, at least one of them headed out through the screen door and down toward the lake, where he had parked, a flashlight held much closer to the ground than is necessary.

August 6

S	M	T	W	T	F	S
1	2	3	4	5	6	7
8	9	10	11	12	13	14
15	16	17	18	19	20	21
22	23	24	25	26	27	28
29	30	31				

19°C. Foggy early, slow to rise. There are reports of bears everywhere from North Bay to Huntsville and all the way over to Ottawa. Interior campers in the Park are being warned as they go in. People say it's the lousy berry crop. Some say it's because they cancelled the spring bear hunt. Others say it's nothing, it's natural. But it sure has everyone around here on guard these days.

Bears at the Dump

It was late summer, the sun slowly sinking in front and the stench of a week's worth of garbage rising fast behind. I was racing to reach the dump before closing and came sliding to a gravel-throwing stop just as Ken, the long-time attendant, was walking the chain-link gate around from the side.

"One minute?" I begged. *"Please."*

Ken stopped just short of snapping the padlock and began walking the gate back into place. "Just make sure you honk when you get to the bins."

I nodded, thinking he meant to time matters so he'd have the gate half-closed by the time I finished. I pulled into a cloud of rising gulls, stepped out, but then remembered Ken's request and leaned in the window to honk.

Suddenly the bin *moved*. First, one small black bear leaped up and out, then a far larger bear rose up like some primordial nightmare and slowly crawled over the edge to stand in front of my vehicle and glower back at me. I shouted. I would like to report that it was a savage, *Braveheart*-like battle cry, but it was more like a missed note by the soloist in a boys' choir. The big bear stared a moment longer, shook its head in dismissal, then ambled off into the pines.

Ken was there when I drove out, padlock poised and grinning ear to ear. "How'd you like my pets?"

It is a fair question and one that cottagers seem rather incapable of answering. Long before the paid attendant and bins, the dump was a summer attraction. Evenings would find cars lining up their high beams in search of a sighting. For city visitors, cringing behind locked doors and rolled-up windows, seeing bears at the dump was a highlight to be treasured. Once they gave dumps office hours, attendants, bins, and silly new names like "transfer stations," the ritual died off and it seemed the bears themselves had moved off. Lately, however, they've come back: Ken counted fourteen different "pets" this summer.

It is foolish to regard them this way, of course. I will never shake the childhood memory of accompanying my ranger grandfather to the Lake of Two Rivers dump, where the nightly bear viewing had gone sadly wrong. A young girl trying to feed cream soda to a cub had been cuffed and, though she'd been uninjured, orders came down to destroy the bears. The rangers shot five adults and two cubs, and I cannot recall ever seeing my grandfather as upset as he was that morning.

But I am also afraid of bears and freely admit it. I have not the courage of the old ranger's wife, my grandmother, who would grab a pot and spoon and charge any bear that came sniffing around her garden. I have seen too often what a hungry bear can do to a pool of suckers, seen their long, spine-tingling scratches on beeches, and have read too many stories about bear attacks not to have a rather healthy respect for them. Others may chuckle at the man who jogs daily down our road with a bear bell jingling from his fanny pack; I don't.

There are around 100,000 black bears in Ontario, and encounters are said to be on the increase. No one seems quite sure why, but it may be nothing more than the natural result of so many more of us heading off into the ever-shrinking bush.

Such encounters have changed opinion on the black bear from when Grey Owl could write in *Tales of an Empty Cabin* that "Your bear is really a good fellow, and will eat most anything that you give him, or that you may inadvertently leave lying around, just to show you that his heart is in the right place."

It's not the bear's *heart* that worries us.

Not that long ago the *Boston Globe* calculated that black bears had killed forty-eight North Americans since 1906, nine of them in Ontario. Not exactly a fearsome track record, as Minnesota wildlife biologist Lynn Rogers pointed out: "People are 42 times more likely to be killed by a domestic dog than a black bear, 120 times more likely to be killed by a bee than a black bear, and 250 times more likely to be killed by lightning."

Those odds are pretty good, and I like seeing bears enough to embrace them. But I also honk when I'm at the bins now—just to improve those odds, however slightly, in my own favour.

Locals versus Tourists

They are telling a new one this summer. After half a
century of Muskoka summers, I have seen and heard
enough to know that, around here, you don't discount any
story, any possibility.

I have seen the snow skis on the roofs of cars with U.S.
licence plates. I was even there the day Huntsville's eccentric inventor Otto Bremer talked the big Toronto newspapers into coming up to watch his Flying Saucer leave this
earthly coil—only to have the first of the four lawn-mower
engines that were to propel the beast he'd built out of
garbage cans and plywood fail to fire, thereby aborting the
official launch.

This year they're telling the one about the busload of
Japanese tourists who pulled up at the dock of a local
Algonquin Park outfitter and how the staff put life
preservers on them, issued each one a paddle, loaded them
into the canoes, one at each end, and then hid behind the
canoe racks holding their guts while the Japanese tried to

figure out how they were supposed to paddle about the bay while they were facing each other.

Apocryphal? Who cares? These stories aren't meant to insult the Japanese any more than the skis are mentioned to ridicule the Americans. They are told, always have been told, and always will be told, to comfort those who come from around here, who are always getting back just a tiny little bit of their own.

To understand Muskoka—to understand, for that matter, so many of the summer tourist playgrounds in this huge, sprawling, city-dominated country—you have to understand the Canadian colonial mentality, and why good, hardworking people can, at times, so deeply resent outsiders who think they can better run everything, from the fur trade to war to, well, daily newspapers.

The early French resented the Crown, the early English resented British Parliament, and later, manufacturers were told what to do by American head offices. Even when the benefits are obvious—and what can be more obvious than the economy created by tourism—there is still an undeniable, abiding emotion that sticks in the craw of those whose livelihood depends on outsiders. Especially so if those outsiders tend to view the locals as support staff, which Muskoka locals more or less are each time summer rolls around.

The defence mechanism is to look down on those who come, before they can look down—as surely they are doing—on those already there. The tourist sees the local as some quaint fauna, wily if not worldly, obscurely philosophical, and endearingly quick to provide humorous anecdotes for dispersal on return to the city.

Locals, of course, have to stay on once the lake turns cold and the first leaves fall. Tourists, therefore, are held not to be particularly bright by the locals. They don't know a snapping turtle from a painted turtle. They would pay, if they could, to see a dump bear rooting around in a rusted dumpster filled with broken green plastic bags—the black bear, in his natural element.

The tourists don't know where the fish are or how to get down to them. They wear short pants into raspberry bushes. They have an endless supply of clean khaki, don't appear to own socks, and—the number one telltale sign of the Modern Outdoors—they wear Tilley hats. (The number two sign, around for decades, is that they refer to this part of the country as "The Muskokas," a phrase that has never, and will never, escape the mouth of a single soul who has passed through a single November or March in Muskoka.)

What tourists do have, however, is a limitless amount of cash and duplicate credit cards. Cottagers like Goldie Hawn and Kurt Russell, American campers, and Japanese tour buses have brought prosperity to places like Muskoka, where, today, even the guy who vents the chemical toilet can afford to vacation in Australia. Tourists also tend to pay their bills, promptly, without complaint—largely because they, it turns out, are at the mercy of the locals as much as the locals are obviously at the mercy of the visitors.

It is a strange, ritualistic, symbiotic relationship. They need each other. They don't always like each other, but they daren't show it. They are, invariably, polite to each other—even if the locals duck behind the canoe racks to howl with laughter and the visitors sit around their cottage campfires each night regaling each other with local accents.

It is a place where both visitor and local laugh at each other behind the other's back. And where neither could exist without the other.

August 8

S	M	T	W	T	F	S
1	2	3	4	5	6	7
⑧	9	10	11	12	13	14
15	16	17	18	19	20	21
22	23	24	25	26	27	28
29	30	31				

27°C. An exquisite day, hot and still and perfect. The mosquitoes are nowhere to be seen and I have run out of excuses. I have put off this job because the earth was frozen, put it off because of blackflies and then mosquitoes, but there is now nothing left to hide behind.

Digging out the Outhouse

"It's a dirty job—but someone's got to do it." I now know I have said that once too often. I say it when people ask me about my newspaper job, which largely amounts to wandering about the country dropping in on everything from elections to Stanley Cup playoffs, but never did I expect someone to throw it back at me. And certainly not here, within sniffing distance of the most run-down building on our otherwise idyllic lakeside property.

For years I had put off the onerous and odorous task of digging out the outhouse, even though it seemed some summers as if Mount Everest, complete with white drifts of toilet paper, were rising from the bedrock and on the verge of poking through the single hole of this homely northern throne.

I put it off with vague promises for years, always thinking I could do it in cold weather, when gas tends not to rise so quickly, and with a tool I could never locate. In the small town where I grew up, the town workers used to clean out storm sewers with long shovels featuring the blade at right angles, and the secret to putting off this pitiful task was to say that I would do it as soon as I found one, which I conveniently never did.

Rot, however, is much like rust, in that it never sleeps. Animals chewed through the walls and the floorboards grew so squishy it seemed but a single hike of the pants before someone plummeted through and was never seen again. And while I did have a list of visitors and family that we could do without, I no longer had the excuse that the outhouse could not be dug out so long as it was absolutely a cottage necessity. We had finally caved in to the pressures of children too aghast to expect city boyfriends and girl-friends to use such a facility and now had a septic system.

The outhouse, in the middle of summer, was idle; so, too, unfortunately, was one of the property owners. The other owner, unfortunately, has no sense of the magic of doing absolutely nothing. She was already at work—levels, two-by-fours, circular saw, hammer and nails—framing in a new outhouse that would, of course, have to go over exactly the same rare digging spot in this particular slab of the Canadian Shield. She would wield the hammer; I would handle the shovelling.

The old outhouse knocked down and carted off to the dump—just try explaining what you've got in the trailer to one of today's "attendants"—I took the longest shovel I could find and set about to dig out the disgusting mess and cart it, in an old washtub, well back into the bush, where I buried it in a sequence of holes known only to me and every animal within five square kilometres.

Working in frantic, two-minute, breath-held shifts, I eventually completed the dastardly deed, maintaining what precious little sanity was left by wondering how it could be that we make so little mention of this place where, one suspects, much of the best thinking in Canadian history has been done by men and women with their pants down around their ankles.

Finished, I contacted the grand collector of all Canadiana, John Robert Colombo, and asked him to ferret through his various *Colombo's Quotations* to see if anything memorable had ever been said about the Great Canadian Outhouse.

Nothing, Colombo reported back. "Perhaps," he suggested, "this says something about the national reserve."

Did I have anything in mind, he wondered?

"It's a dirty job," I began ...

The Annual
Canoe Trip

There is a time of year, late winter, when I should be committed. It sometimes seems that the only thing my curious behaviour lacks is Oliver Sacks, the famous neurologist and bestselling author, sitting in the corner, taking notes as I go about my strange and mysterious business.

I run my hand along the side of the canvas canoe as if it were a family pet—which, in an odd way, it is. I take my paddle and practise the "J" stroke against the air. I check rope and gear and tent pegs and packsacks and tarpaulins with the loving care of an orchid grower making the rounds of his greenhouse, my watering can my own imagination.

I pore over maps. Not maps of Route 95 to Florida or the Trans-Canada Highway headed east or west, but *Canoe Routes of Algonquin Provincial Park,* using an adding machine to tally up portages and a calendar to work out what is possible for the various members of a busy family of six. I then take out my credit card, dial 1-888-ONT-PARK, and book what has increasingly become a major cottage project for each coming summer. A brief escape from escape.

I am not a hammer and nails person. I do not wear a tape measure, as some do, as if it were attached at birth. I look at empty space and see empty space, not bunkies or deck extensions or sheds. But do not think I am without my ambitious summer projects. Mine are adventures. Biking around the lake. Hiking in to an isolated body of water with nothing but a topographical map and a compass. And, of course, making the annual getaway from the cottage.

This is, I know, a difficult one to explain and has nothing whatsoever to do with trying to avoid the cottage. It is, instead, about *appreciating* the cottage all the more. It grows out of something our son, Gord, once said at the end of yet another summer when we had contrived to spend every conceivable second we could at the lake.

"Next summer," he said, "I want to do some different things at the cottage. I don't like it when I look back and it all seems the same."

He was speaking, of course, from the viewpoint of the Life Cycle of the Lake Teenager: sleep in, get up, put on bathing suit, fall off end of dock, eat, head out in boat, visit, dive off rocks, hang around, eat, fish, swim, play, build campfire, stay up too late, eat, sleep ... Something was needed to break the pattern. Day trips were fine, but the real breakthrough came the summer we all headed off into the Park to spend the better part of a week exploring where their grandparents and great-grandparents had once lived their entire lives.

The planning was exhausting. I assigned myself the task of staring at the map and daydreaming, while Ellen took on arranging the equipment, planning the food, ironing out the dates, and finding Zip-Lock bags big enough to hold several rolls of toilet paper. Several weeks later we launched the three canoes and headed off toward the first portage in what, over the next several days, would become our full-time, dawn-to-dusk jobs.

We loved it, of course. There is something about what American naturalist John Muir calls "this sudden plash into wilderness" that creates fresh appreciation for what we presume, wrongly, we already appreciate enough. We made plans for the whole family to go together, but then had to adjust when, at the last minute, oldest daughter Kerry was unfortunately prevented from coming by work obligations. But Christine, Jocelyn, and Gordon were still on, and Kerry's place was taken by Jocelyn's friend, James. Three canoes, two tents, six packsacks, and slightly less than a million dollars worth of powdered gourmet food requiring only water, a little heat, and a lot of imagination.

Ellen and I set off thinking we would be carrying the load. We, after all, had the experience. We travelled through lakes and rivers and up wrong creeks and over portages so short it seemed we could throw the packs, then over portages so long it seemed we were leaving Ontario to put in at Saskatchewan.

We worked from dawn to dusk—tents to put up and break down, fires to build, food to cook, and dishes to wash—and spent each evening around the campfire talking and laughing as perhaps we had never done before. We heard stories we couldn't believe, told stories we couldn't believe we were telling, and probably got to know our children better in less than a week than we had in the previous decade.

We had come into the bush believing we were the leaders; by the third day it was clear we were no longer in charge, but merely following our children, who had somehow become their own persons: young and confident adults even more anxious to see what lay around the next bend than we were ourselves.

It was not intended to be a particularly difficult trip, but it was most assuredly intended to be a significant one. It took these children—no, these young adults—into the heart of the country where their recently lost grandmother had been born and spent the first seventeen years of her life. At roughly the same ages they now were, she would have canoed these same waters. She had lived with her family at Brule Lake, a tiny Park community that is now nothing more than a few foundation logs and a vague sense that a railway line had once passed through these parts.

She had been born, her older sister once recalled, on a similar hot August day back in 1915, in a summer tent where they dipped blankets in these waters and strung them, dripping, over cross poles to cool the tent down while her mother, the great-grandmother of these youngsters, went into labour.

We wanted them to know these things. We wanted them to know that Algonquin Park runs through their veins as surely as the Petawawa and the Madawaska rivers run through the Park itself. Their great-grandfather was a ranger all his working life, their grandfather a logger here for more than half a century. Both worked into their seventies and both were forced to quit—one by the ministry, one by a sliding wood chip truck—jobs from which they never took vacations. As far as the old ranger and old logger were concerned, if you were lucky enough to work in this part of the country, there was nothing you ever wanted to get away from.

We wanted these young people to know about the lives of their grandmother Helen and great-aunt Mary and their great-grandmother Bea, a tiny Irish tornado who couldn't swim a stroke yet canoed through these lakes and rivers as effortlessly as those loons in the near bay move along as they look for minnows. We wanted them to feel as if they owned the Park and yet know that no one owns the Park, which is why any such designated wilderness has no meaningful value anyone can put on it. We hoped they would take possession of it, and they did, and then realized that in fact the opposite had taken place: the Park now possessed them.

We all had to go on this trip together, as it is simply not possible to bring an experience like this home. Like those roadside photographs of moose that come back showing only black shadows, it is difficult to impart to others what it is to be so close to nature, to hear wolves howl at night and yet never feel so safe and secure in your life.

There is no way for a human to pass on the sound of a loon as darkness falls. No way to describe what the water looks like at dawn when you shiver out of a tent and watch mist shift as if it's about to part like a curtain and let Tom Thomson himself paddle through from another time.

We rediscovered, as the days rolled into each other, the delight of our own conversation, when too often the telephone, the radio, or that cursed single-channel cottage television takes talk away. We gained a renewed respect for the simplicity of the outdoor life, the joy of very small things, and when we came out, even after such a short time, we felt the way distant travellers do when they return to Canada, everything under a new light with new meaning.

For us, it was a welcome—and now an annual—reminder of the original purpose of the summer cottage. To get close to nature.

August 28

S M T W T F S
1 2 3 4 5 6 7
8 9 10 11 12 13 14
15 16 17 18 19 20 21
22 23 24 25 26 27 (28)
29 30 31

21°C. Rain during night. Holding off, if barely, in the morning. Summer is starting to close down and you can feel it everywhere. I think even the dog knows. Every summer it's the same story around this time of the month. No one wants to admit it's over; everyone knows it's almost over.

The Cat Who Went Missing

She was ten years old that distant summer—raspberry-scratched, tar-footed, band-aided, sunburnt, and even more freckled than when she arrived in mid-July—and she was hanging from the window of a dust-covered vehicle going down the fifth dirt road of the morning and she was screaming at the top of her lungs:

"This is all a dream!"

We were looking for the cat. For two days we had been looking for the cat and finding nothing but more dirt roads and more deep, dark, silent bush to scream into—a brief, passing advertisement for the insanity of city life.

"This has got to be a dream!"

She was shouting at summer, a summer slipping away from us all. I was thinking more in terms of a nightmare—the $30,000 or so worth of new lures now hanging on the bottom of the lake. Her two older sisters were thinking about their new friends, the campfires, the fifty-foot rope one of them had tied to the highest branch of the old yellow birch hanging out over the water and the free ride that had, all summer long, been the talk of the lake.

The boy was still counting the ten largest bass in the history of the world, all unfortunately lost to science by a hapless adult who either forgot the net/couldn't reach the net in time/tied the leader on too loosely/wouldn't buy thirty-pound test line/didn't see it jump/or kicked the fish off the edge of the dock when it spit out the hook.

The dog (barely a puppy this summer) had finally learned to swim when someone threw her off the dock and now wouldn't come out unless there was a dry towel to shake over.

There was even, finally, some evidence that reading Archie comics does not necessarily turn the mind to mouse nest. The oldest was now sunning with Margaret Laurence, though it would be unfair to compare her reading level to the adult sitting in the hammock with *News of the World*.

He, you might need to know, is by now utterly convinced that somewhere there is a chimpanzee with a transplanted human brain, a perfectly formed and healthy baby only three inches long, and a man who charges spectators to watch him blow cigarette smoke through a hole in his back.

It had, so far, been the typical perfect summer. But then, on a morning when the sun was once again at the door looking for someone to play with, someone had noticed something was missing.

"Have you seen the cat lately?"

No one had, but when they thought about it they did think it had been some days since they had run barefoot up to the outhouse and had to side-step the night's slaughter of shrew.

For a day we waited, often looking and periodically calling, then panicked. The kids made up posters and nailed them up at the government dock. We called the nearest animal shelter; the local radio station put out notice. We started patrolling the back roads, the youngest daughter calling the cat's name until she was hoarse and could only wail into the bush: *It has to be a dream!* But nothing. No calls. No sightings.

Cats being so different from dogs, no one quite knew what to do. The dog you would notice missing with the arrival of the first guest: no jumping up with dirty paws, no crotch sniffing. But who could say how long a cat might be gone before someone noticed? And when had she ever come to a call?

By the time the third day rolled around since her absence had been noticed, the adults were convinced of the worst. There was even a tramp through the bush to see if a wild animal had won a battle with her, a check of the road-side for an accident. On the final evening, with school looming and the city insisting, the younger children went to bed in tears.

And then, at precisely 3:05 A.M. on the very last day, there was this arrogant, angry *"meow"* outside the window. The door opened and the cat walked in as if nothing whatsoever had happened—like Agatha Christie, her brief disappearance never to be explained.

In the morning the kids had acted as if she were a new kitten, wrapping her in towels and carrying her about as if she were a doll. The ten-year-old had hugged the indignant cat and decided, very surely: "Maybe it *was* a dream!" She meant the cat's disappearance, of course. But to some of us, it sounded like summer itself.

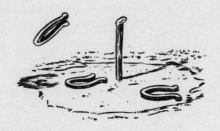

Labour Day Weekend

I am almost at the end of my rope. Well, technically, at the end of daughter Christine's rope—after all, she's the one who shinnied up this massive yellow birch a number of years ago and tied it around the largest branch hanging out over the bay.

The rope is famous, from one end of this little Canadian Shield lake to the other. On those hot summer days when all anyone can think about is getting wet and staying wet, they come from all over to swing high out over the sun-dappled bay and drop, children cheering and dog barking, into water so cool and clear it seems the essence of the sweetest season itself. This, however, is September. A moment ago, two youngsters from down the shore churned and gurgled by in a paddleboat, thick sweatshirts sticking out from under their life preservers.

"Been in yet?" I called.

One shook his baseball cap violently. "Too cold," he giggled.

They paddled on, staring back as if I had gone temporarily insane.

It is not temporary. I am past fifty. I open and end each swimming season with the same swing out over the water and drop into the unexpected. If I can do it at eighty—if the rope still holds and the yellow birch and I are still standing—I will count it as a life well lived.

This is both the saddest time of the year and the most exciting, a time when one treasured life comes to an end and one necessary life picks up again. It is a moment of shock, not unlike a hard slap to the face or, depending on how I turn in the air, the bottom—so it is not that much of an exaggeration to think of it as being reborn, even if reluctantly.

The rope in question is half an inch thick and hangs from a yellow birch down near the water's edge. It was tied by Christine, who, as a high-tower diver having no fear of heights, shinnied up with the plastic rope in her teeth, tied it, and then completed a back two-and-a-half-with-a-full-twist into the middle of the bay—or so the story goes around the campfires.

No matter. The rope is still holding fast, the yellow birch still standing when so many of the hemlocks and cedars have fallen to wind or lightning. Halfway up the hill to the cottage there is a launching platform to give the insane that little extra height to send them flying out over the bay in a long, slow arc that ends, some twenty feet over the water, when the hands finally let go and the body, according to inclination, can either drop straight down or spin into whatever belly flop or backslap comes of it.

The water is always the same temperature, first and last dive of the year. And yet, in late May or early June, it seems so filled with promise, in early September so filled with regret. This is the time of year when we notice the changes. From a distance, the baby loon is hard to pick out from the parents. No one is going barefoot any longer, and sometimes in the early morning you are convinced you can see your breath.

The lake has turned over. No one saw it happen. No one heard it happen. There was no roar, no wave, no notice posted by the government dock. Still, the lake has turned over and is suddenly a stranger. It no longer invites you in. The lake is silver-plated and dull now where gold is supposed to dance over a teasing blue. It seems it would repel now instead of refresh, and a dive now requires a long series of commands, internal debates, and a final, heartless push rather than merely giving in to the curious magnetic pull created when a northern lake and a southern sun are so briefly in the correct alignment.

What happened? Carefully, you recite the Canadian creed: *This is a wonderful country we live in, we are so fortunate to be able to enjoy all the seasons, fall is the most glorious time of the year, I can hardly wait for winter ...*

The end of summer must be accepted so one can get on with fall and winter and into spring, and, before you know it, you lucky Canadian, summer will be able to begin again. *And again be over with the snap of a finger,* the beast within snarls. These final plunges into summer, of course, are to drown the beast. Once a Canadian body strikes end-of-summer water, the Canadian mind is able to accept, finally, that it is indeed all over and there is absolutely nothing you can do about it. So quit sulking.

Personally, I have come to look upon Labour Day Weekend as the real Canadian New Year, the true demarcation line that signals the end of one good run and the start of another. Who, really, can tell the difference between December 31 and January 1? Both are white, cold, and, unless you remembered to plug in, you aren't going anywhere anyway. But who does not feel the profound shift between Labour Day and the long, sad drive back to school and work?

This, not December 31, is when Canadians make their resolutions—to get in shape, to remember priorities, to pull in the docks before the ice pulls them out—and this, too, is when most of us feel like getting drunk and sloppy and singing stupid, sad songs.

But first we must complete the final swing of summer. The legs push off, finally, and the trees blur—but not so much that you do not catch the creeping colour—and the air carries but the slightest hint of fall. The water, however, is the colour of pewter, and it seems, for a moment, as if you might bounce right off it if you drop. But then everything stops for the brief instant when momentum and gravity cancel each other out. There's only you, summer hanging by a thread, and no choice but to give in to the laws of nature. And drop back into the life you left a few short but glorious weeks ago.

September 10

S	M	T	W	T	F	S
			1	2	3	4
5	6	7	8	9	⑩	11
12	13	14	15	16	17	18
19	20	21	22	23	24	25
26	27	28	29	30		

23°C. I sometimes wonder why people talk about the five—or is it seven?—stages of death and don't apply the same to summer. It's been weeks since the panic set in, weeks even since acceptance set in. And this September, so far, has been the sweetest of all the good months, warmer than either July or August, more sun than June despite the shorter daylight hours. It's been most pleasant, and each weekend we have found ourselves deciding, at the last moment, to head up just for the weekend because, well, the forecast is great.

The Official
Canadian Bug Off

We are entering the second lull. It happens but twice a
year and, in a subtle way, poses the question as to how
Canadians can *stand* the rest of the year. It is when the
weather is absolutely lovely, the sun warm, and the air soft,
and not a bug to be seen.

I took note of this phenomenon in the early spring
when, during a week off at the lake, I discovered there
exists a magical time, however brief, when the sun is out
but the leaves are not, when the ice has vanished but the
blackflies have yet to appear. A very rough description
might be heaven on earth.

It is about to happen again. The bugs have mostly died
off and autumn can be the most wonderful time of year to
be at a cottage—a time when it is possible to dance in the
high grass and weed back of the outhouse and not be
swarmed by a single thing but seed.

It has been said this year that the blackflies were the
worst ever, then that the mosquitoes were the worst

ever—almost as if this precious lakeshore property had suddenly become a combination dung heap, garbage dump, and slaughterhouse. And so I am left at the end of a year in which Canadians decided who was the worst political party trying to determine which, in fact, is the worst bug. Let us, then, begin The Official Canadian Bug Off.

The Blackfly: Has the distinct advantage of being the first bug to follow winter, the one, essentially, that ruins everything. Too small to see accurately, too thick to destroy completely, it can crawl into holes you did not even know your body has. Its bite is worse in the scratching, and bites sometimes become infected, especially in the scalps of small children. Blackflies have been known to drive moose into traffic and early explorers as well as early gardeners insane. Their one positive feature is that one day in late spring they suddenly, and mysteriously, vanish.

The Mosquito: This country's true national symbol. Not the beaver. Its bite is so sharp that humans have been known to injure themselves slapping back. Its most annoying attribute, however, is sound, sound growing and sound suddenly stopping—landing location unknown! Since the arrival of the West Nile virus—cottagers can only shake their heads at the radio ads suggesting mosquitoes be avoided and standing water eliminated—their annoyance level has taken a quantum leap.

The Ankle Biter: Also known as the stable fly. A relatively recent phenomenon, they appear like small houseflies but only around bare ankles in canoes and boats. Their bite is roughly equivalent to a match bursting into flame just beneath your skin, and panic swatting, in a canoe, makes them doubly dangerous.

The Deerfly: If you were a dog with floppy ears, this would be no contest. The bite of the deerfly is roughly the equivalent of dropping a running chainsaw on your fleshy parts. They alone know the secret passage that leads below baseball caps. They are, mercifully, the fly with the lowest IQ, meaning you can usually pluck one out of your hair and squeeze it as slowly as revenge requires.

The Horsefly: The swimmer's curse. Their bite is the insect world's answer to the Great White Shark. One does not get "bitten" by a horsefly as much as "kicked." The one saving grace is that, like cottage country bargains, there are not many of them.

We must, therefore, now declare a winner in this first annual Canadian Bug Off. It is, of course, the next one that lands on you.

Car Hits Bear

If one moment stands out from these many difficult weeks of unforced vacation, it would have to be that early Sunday morning along the gravel road heading into Achray Station when I hit the bear.

We were headed off on a short canoe trip down the Barron River that runs through a spectacular canyon along the eastern edge of Algonquin Park; he was headed off in search of blueberries or whatever it is exactly that bears do in the woods; and our mutual timing couldn't have been more unfortunate.

I saw him coming at the last second. He saw me coming— or at least the truck I was wearing at the time—too late. I slammed on the brakes. He paused once, then bolted directly in front of the oncoming bumper. Fortunately, I was not going very fast and he was very fat. There was not even a sound to be heard as the bumper clipped his butt and sent him flying through the air in a perfect somersault.

Animals, we are told, are not capable of facial expressions, but let science record that, in this particular case, an entire screen test of shock, surprise, confusion, disappointment, and, ultimately, relief registered on the face of a young black bear crossing the dirt road to Achray. He landed like a seasoned high jumper, rolled once in a cloud of dry gravel, kipped up to all fours, and scrambled off before the truck could even come to a full stop.

I got out and we stood for a long moment staring at each other. He shook his head once, seemed almost to shrug the whole thing off, and ambled off into the trees as if this near tragedy had never even happened. In this country, you take your metaphors where you find them.

A man on the north shore of the lake where we spent so much of July and August called this "The Summer That Wasn't" after his three weeks of holidays hit little but north winds and talk about whether or not it was going to rain. He headed back to fire-stricken British Columbia, where they were then still dealing with "The Summer That Shouldn't Have Been."

I was headed back to Ottawa in the same week that the federal government declared there will be no more smiling on passports. It had been that kind of summer. I went into the bush this particular summer to escape a country reeling from SARS, mad-cow disease, and West Nile virus, and came out to find that the power was off in Ontario and British Columbia was on fire. I left a job where, tradition-ally, news takes its own vacation in summer and returned to a newspaper desperate for a break, any break, from natural disasters, possible terrorists flying over Canadian nuclear stations, and people supposedly falling ill from eating bad meat.

They are calling whatever it is the world is going through "the new normal," and for several days I was delighted to be lost in the old normal: worrying about raccoons getting into food packs, surprising two fawns that had come to drink at the shore of Stratton Lake, turning a corner on the river to find a moose casually dining on water lily, laughing as a family of otters formed a chattering, squeaking convoy to see our canoes through the canyon.

There was no radio to turn on, no newspaper landing on the campsite before 6:30 A.M., no cellphones, no email, no news save that of other campers talking about bears along the portages. It was a summer to gain new appreciation for American writer Annie Dillard's marvellous line about heading for Hollins Pond near her West Coast home "not so much to learn how to live as, frankly, to forget about it."

Shortly it will be time again to head off to school, sign up for sports, enroll in courses, start new jobs, start looking for new jobs, launch new projects, and make our annual resolutions to get fit or smarter—whatever it takes to shake off the slack months just past and start afresh.

The bear picked himself right up and kept on going, just as if that bump in the road had never happened. Not a bad example for the rest of the country.

September 18

S	M	T	W	T	F	S
			~~1~~	~~2~~	~~3~~	~~4~~
~~5~~	~~6~~	~~7~~	~~8~~	~~9~~	~~10~~	~~11~~
~~12~~	~~13~~	~~14~~	~~15~~	~~16~~	~~17~~	⑱
19	20	21	22	23	24	25
26	27	28	29	30		

17°C and bright. Drove up in beautiful weather to see the leaves. Algonquin Park is like a traffic jam and the colours are still at least two weeks away from peak. We stopped for ice cream at the Canoe Lake store, and if you just sat in the sun by the dock licking your cone you could pick up several different languages—Japanese being the majority, German a close second—and a dozen different North American accents. This time of year, getting there can be more than half the fun.

Maps

Perhaps this fall I will get back to Lost Nation. I am talking not about the simple country Prime Minister Louis St. Laurent once governed, but Lost Nation, that little speck on the map off the Letterkenny Road that runs north of Quadeville, just off the 513.

A couple of years ago I got as far as the secret log hideaway of Al Capone—you know, the Chicago mobster who once claimed "I don't even know what *street* Canada's on," even though local lore claims he hid out near Quadeville in the 1940s—but stopped short of Lost Nation and only came across it again while reading a map of eastern Ontario one rainy weekend at the cottage.

Strange, isn't it, how we talk about "settling down with a good book" but never talk about the huge pleasures of reading a map and wondering what it would be like to head out in search of places with names that suggest stories that should, perhaps, be books.

There is, in an old dresser drawer in this cabin, a topographical map that has fascinated three generations—names like Pinfeather Lake and Distress Dam that call out to be seen, a place like the Big East River that sounds like it belongs in a Hemingway short story.

The cottage itself is at the farthest end of what I have always believed to be an absolutely mystical name for a country road: Limberlost. I'm not sure exactly what it means—there was once a romantic novel called *Limberlost Girl* or something—but to those who turn onto Limberlost Road on a Friday night, it means everything.

I can sit down with nothing so much as a dog-eared and torn provincial road map and, by searching through print smaller than no-see-ums, come upon spots like Buttermilk Falls in Haliburton and Bridal Veil Falls on the Manitoulin and be instantly swept back to long-ago camping trips and Sunday afternoon drives.

With that topographical map of our cottage area—Energy, Mines and Resources Canada No. 31 E/7—I can imagine heading due south down an ancient logging road, conveniently marked by dotted line, crossing one rise of land listed at 1500 feet above sea level, another at 1350 feet, and eventually reaching the banks of the Oxtongue River near Ragged Falls.

I know I am not alone when it comes to this passion for maps. An atlas can hold me entranced for hours. When I travel across this vast country for work, which is fairly often, I am never so happy as when I turn the rental car out the airport entrance and realize I have no idea what lies around the first turn.

But nothing compares to those topographical maps or the provincial park publications that show canoe routes and backpacking trails. They are what Wilderness Society founder Bob Marshall was getting at when he spoke of an abiding passion for "blank spaces on maps." When we strike out for them, we are, for the moment, all explorers.

Please do not take from this that I have the slightest sense of direction. I am, after all, a male, and though I will never ask for directions I have been known, at times, to pray for them.

I suspect this love of beckoning trails comes from the old Algonquin Park ranger who spent much of his retirement taking grandchildren off into the bush to retrace his working hikes to isolated lakes and abandoned logging camps. He could read blazes on trees better than I can read city street maps, and as we hiked in he would always leave fresh blazes. Not once do I recall his being unsure of where he was going or where, exactly, he would end up.

I now carry a compass—a gift from daughter Jocelyn, who is as passionate about the wild as her ranger great-grandfather—but have yet to take the modern leap to a hand-held global positioning system. At the moment, anyway, it strikes me as a little too close to "cheating," using billions of dollars worth of satellite gear to keep track of a happy wanderer who should be able to work things out for himself with a compass, a map, and that most elusive of all qualities—a little common sense.

The dog-eared road map tells me that Lost Nation is south of Brudenell and north of where they claim Al Capone holed up one summer and even had a secret underground escape tunnel. It's also east of Pilgrims Creek and west of Yukes Lake. (Don't you just love the names?) I'll take along my new compass and the old map, of course. And perhaps even a hatchet to leave the odd blaze along the way. Just in case.

Dog Years and Human Years

"You will know when it's time."

Fine, but how? There is no expiry date on her that I can find, nothing at all to indicate shelf life apart from the obvious fact that she was clearly "best before" any of this came along. There is no timely reminder in the mail, no message on the answering machine, no waiter discreetly laying her plastic card on the table and whispering that it is no longer considered "active." She would take offence to that.

This is approximately the sixth time since May that we have come here together so she can spend her final days where she has always been happiest. I carry her to the car, place her in a backseat specifically set up so she cannot fall off and get stuck anywhere—and yet several times each drive I will have to stop and adjust her. One time it will be her back legs stuck between seat and door; another time she will be wedged head first between back seat and front seat.

She never says anything. Of course, it has been a year now since she last barked. Hard to believe, since it was always her wild, excited barking that announced we were here, the way others might hoist a flag. What is totally mysterious is how this old dog, who cannot see, who cannot hear, still manages to wobble to her four feet when the car turns onto the long country road that leads in here, and how the panting that would have been described as "laboured" only hours earlier is now almost puppylike.

"You will know when it's time."

They all say that. And surely, I thought when we headed out, this will be it. There is a shovel leaning against the cabin. There is a place picked out back in the bush by a huge rock this mutt—sort of "borderline collie"—could once bounce onto in a single leap. Now, however, she needs to be carried down the three small steps leading from the door to where she awkwardly does the required business and then needs carrying back up again.

I used to be baffled by stories such as the one about legendary hockey coach Roger Neilson pushing his old mutt around in a shopping cart because the dog could no longer walk and Roger could not do what needed to be done, but now I understand. Fifteen years ago when this mutt was a puppy we bought a cage that resembled a shopping cart without wheels. The idea was to place the dog in it when we went out. The first time we tried it we came home and found all four kids inside the cage with the puppy happily bouncing off it as she tried to get at them. They just didn't want to deal with her frenetic energy. Now they have trouble dealing with her lack of energy and are happy to carry her up and down the steps, more than willing to pick her up when she falls.

The end of a pet is one of the great curiosities of society. Within the family walls, it is devastating. One step beyond those walls it means little; two steps, nothing.

I never expected her to last this long. She wouldn't make the May 24th weekend ... she wouldn't make Canada Day ... she wouldn't make Labour Day ... now we say she won't make Thanksgiving.

But summer did not come to this part of the country until early fall—just as the Sixties didn't reach Canada until sometime in the early Seventies—and so here she is, still sniffing around the pine needles, still heading instinctively down toward the water. Only with such a difference. Whereas once it was full bore down the hill and off the end of the dock, now it might be slipping and rolling down the hill and falling in.

It helps to remember that this old dog—now so skinny, now so helpless—once was the talk of the lake as she was known to swim entirely across it if she heard children swimming and figured she'd better round them up and head them back to shore.

"You will know when it's time."

I suppose this is true enough. We knew when it was time the last time this situation had to be faced.

The lake is remarkably calm, unlike the man standing at the end of the dock wondering what to do, and when to do it.

The old dog is at the steps, determined. She locks the back legs that no longer seem to work and hops once, slipping but holding, hops again and is down on her own, blindly heading into a world of a thousand nasal delights. There is, perhaps unintentional, also a slight bounce to her step. And perhaps the man at the end of the dock misreads it. But so what? It is not time yet.

Not yet.

September 26

S M T W T F S
1 2 3 4
5 6 7 8 9 10 11
12 13 14 15 16 17 18
19 20 21 22 23 24 25
(26) 27 28 29 30

12° C. Bright and still, if cold; the leaves glorious. Ellen and I came over for the weekend to make sure everything was in order and to top up the woodpile for winter, presuming we will get here a few times through the snow. Nothing worse than coming in at 20° below and finding an empty wood box.

The Woodpile

These are the days of the morning fire, when getting the chill out of the air is as much a cottage priority as a quick swim, a cold beer, and a good mystery novel were just a few short weeks ago.

It is fall, when the cottage woodpile takes on new meaning and added value, when a lack of kindling can cause panic and wet, green wood can turn the air blue with more than smoke.

We take our woodpiles mostly for granted, forgetting entirely about them for long stretches through both summer and winter, and yet it is astonishing what the gathering, storing, and use of firewood can tell you about both cottagers and visitors.

If you suspect a guest has been a trifle boastful about his wilderness prowess—the reference to males is deliberate; women never brag about such matters—simply hand him an axe and ask him to split a bit of wood while you pretend to do something like level the dock. And then, from a convenient hideaway, watch. By the swing of the axe ye shall know him.

Guests who use your cabin when you are not there can also be measured far better by the wood stock than by any thank-you bottle of wine. The wood box should be replenished perfectly, the kindling stashed high and dry and finely split with a clear understanding between the relative combustion values of hemlock and cedar. An empty kindling bin and depleted wood box are legally acceptable grounds for never extending another invitation.

No Canadian has ever been as identified with woodpiles as much as was legendary journalist Bruce Hutchison, who died several years ago at the age of ninety-one. Hutchison often claimed he could never have survived editing the *Winnipeg Free Press, Victoria Times,* and *Vancouver Sun* were it not for the therapeutic value of a sharp axe and the chopping block.

Not long before the old newspaperman's death, I visited him in his Victoria home and was as keen to see his axe as I was to stare at the typewriter on which he'd written such classics as *The Unknown Country.* Hutchison, to his credit, openly acknowledged his obsession. "Like tobacco, drink and drugs," he wrote in his memoirs, "wood can be an incurable addiction, and it had long held me in its grip."

Hutchison and his wife, Dot, had a cabin retreat at Shawnigan Lake on Vancouver Island, a rustic little spot where he went, deliberately, to avoid the news of the day, and he spent so much of his spare time cutting, chopping, and piling that he became almost as famous in the bush for his axe as he was in the journalism world for his words.

"According to local gossip," he happily conceded, "my secret woodpiles along the forest paths were uncounted, forgotten and decayed. Percy Rawling denounced me as a miser and alleged that I never gave my wife the best-quality wood for her kitchen stove. 'She'd only burn it,' I was quoted as saying. Percy spread the slander until Dot almost came to believe him."

It is a lovely story, and one to which all of us who treasure our woodpiles, our rhythmic hours of chopping, our less-than-perfect piling, and our endless search for dry kindling can relate.

The old Park ranger used to look so perfectly at ease cutting cedar kindling that, to this day, I will try and stand and swing just like him, choking up on the axe and seeming only to "tap" the wood so it splits, the wonderful cedar aroma exploding out of each punch like a small reward for a job well done. I cannot, however, cut hardwood as he did, with a deft little flick of the wrist at the precise moment the head of the axe struck the block of maple or ash, the wood fracturing with a distinctive "pop"—almost as if it had been bound with elastic and merely waiting for him to come along and release it.

But if the style of the chopper can tell so much, so, too, can the result. My parents used to admire fine woodpiles the way, today, we might drive along noting country gardens or ponds, or even three-car garages. A friend who grew up in the bush says her father would make them pile the wood so carefully that there would be enough space for a squirrel to scramble through, but not the cat chasing it.

The last observation we must leave to Bruce Hutchison, on the woodshed: "It contains not just some fuel but nearly all that mankind has learned, so far, about civilized society."

I wouldn't go that far. But I certainly will go some.

"Progress" Comes to the Lake

I am sitting at the oilcloth-covered kitchen table with the local Yellow Pages open to "Septic Systems"—on the verge of making a call we said for years we would never make—and I cannot help but be struck by how so much around here has snuck up on us over the years.

It would be unfair to call what has taken place escalation, for the only thing we are at war with is our own sentimental notion of what a cottage should be; but it would be fair to call it attrition, for it has all happened so slowly it has been barely noticed as the summers slide by—a sort of innocent *wearing away* of good intention that, by the time it is finally recognized for what it is, may already be too late.

Just look around here. I am about to use a telephone, the absence of which was, at one point, considered a pleasure so great at this cottage that it could be compared, roughly, to the delight of rounding a turn in the creek at the end of the lake and chancing upon a feeding moose.

In the thirty-year history of this small, simple, rustic cottage, the first half was passed without any form of communication apart from a twenty-minute drive toward town for the first available pay phone. No one ever died. One day in the early 1980s, however, we installed a simple, black rotary telephone on a party line for, we argued, "safety reasons." The cottage, which was built by Ellen's parents, was then solely in the hands of Ellen's mother, a vibrant and independent, but obviously aging, woman who insisted on spending time alone where she and her husband had passed their best times of all. *She could fall ... We can check up on her ... It would be handy ...* All the predictable rationalizations, with all the predictable results.

Nothing happened to her; it happened to us. Over time, the number was gradually passed on so far beyond family that it eventually ended up with work, the very caller I was once so delighted to avoid. The *Toronto Star,* my then employer, turned to small, now-hopelessly-inadequate laptop computers and asked if I would care to be the first guinea pig. Quicker than a modern modem, a new—and highly dangerous—thought had raced to the brain: *I could work from the cottage.*

That was twenty years ago. The "emergency" phone is gone, its rotary dial no good for computers. It is no longer a party line, Bell Canada having realized that once a phone line gets into a cottage, it is more likely than mice to stay and multiply. There are two phone jacks in the wall. We have yet to put in a separate line for high-speed data transmission, but who knows what insanity will strike next?

Perhaps in this interval between Closing Up and Opening Up again—for those of us who still honour such practices—we should all step back a moment and look, with the advantage of distance, at what we have done to our most treasured possession.

I can recall a local cottagers' association meeting many years ago where an older, white-bearded man put forward the notion that some of these smaller lakes near Algonquin Park should be restricted to canoes only, and personally it seemed to me a fine, if unworkable, notion.

I had no idea then that I would evolve into the very creature he so clearly wished to avoid. But we had two very young children then, and now there are four, and somewhere along the way they hit the teenage years, and before we knew it we had to build a separate shed down by the water just to hold the ropes and boards and tubes and—*good heavens! Where did that 90-horsepower boat with the wakeboard bar come from?* We have two floating docks and they are not enough.

I no longer show up for the annual cottagers' meetings. I am too ashamed. And yet, I am not all that much different from our neighbours, who have also been metamorphosing into new and strange creatures never before found on these lakes. A man along the south shore has been known to hike up the high hill back of his rustic cottage—no electricity, no running water—and attempt to use his cellphone for business so he can whittle a few more days into his vacation.

There are now a few cottages wearing the telltale metal dishes indicating that, on any given summer's evening, the vacationers now have a choice between 160 movies, 56 sporting events—or the sunset.

We, too, brought a small black-and-white television to the cottage. It came from a garage sale ($10) and was rationalized, as all new electronic arrivals are, as something that *made sense*—though, of course, it makes none whatsoever. The kids could hook up their Nintendo, and did, but soon I, too, was pulling it out to watch hockey during the March Break. So what if it looked like they were playing in a blizzard? *Old time hockey!*

When the horizontal started to go, we took the next obvious step down the slippery slope. We picked up a small, cheap, colour set that—aha!—just happens to have a VCR built in to it so that now we, too, can watch the latest Tom Cruise instead of going for one up around the far bay where the loons have their nest and are teaching the little one to dive. Ancestors, forgive me for what I have done—and, for that matter, what I am planning to do.

It would be easier if we could just blame Benjamin Franklin, Thomas Edison, and Alexander Graham Bell for what has happened to cottage country over the past quarter-century, but all of us know this would be no better than blaming Cadbury for our cavities.

We may have, almost by accident, become our own worst enemies. Mass transportation first made cottage country more accessible to more people. Prosperity, even limited, made a place at the lake within reach, and better roads and vehicles shortened that reach. Electricity reduced the effort and helped, along with better insulation, snowmobiles, and four-wheel-drive SUVs, to extend the season to the point where it now potentially wraps around the entire calendar year. Telephones opened up communication—unfortunately, we may one day conclude, in both directions.

There is something terribly worrisome about this rush to bring the conveniences of home and the inconveniences of the office to the bush. It seems to go against all that we have always felt about the very nature of escape, even if we have not always been able to articulate what we mean by getting away, periodically, from the overwhelming bulk of our lives. In stretching the time spent at the lake so thinly, we risk tearing the very fabric that makes up the summer delight.

"I love it," the American writer John Irving wrote of a visit to Georgian Bay in *A Prayer for Owen Meany*. "For a short time, it is soothing. I can almost imagine that I have had a life very different from the life I have had." Plug in that fax machine, however, or put in an extra phone jack for the modem, and the life at the lake is increasingly in danger of becoming very *similar* to the life left behind. The office, with blackflies.

It was not so long ago—and there are still many who believe this—that the very lack of convenience of the cottage was considered a large part of its appeal. Coal oil lamps, wood fires, buckets of water from the lake, the outhouse—all were held up as welcome reminders of where we came from, in both possible definitions. It put us out of touch with the city, and in touch with our heritage, and surely there is at least a small betrayal here when we compare our concerns over satellite reception and download time to those whose greatest worries were blackened chimney glass and whether or not they had enough three-inch nails on hand.

That, surely, is what Thoreau was getting at when he said he took to the woods in order "to live deliberately, to front only the essential facts of life, and see if I could not learn what it had to teach, and not, when I came to die, discover that I had not lived."

The question is: if we truly feel more *alive* at the cottage, as we so readily claim, what is it here that makes the blood flow differently? The necessity of work? The joy of simple tasks? The lack of distraction that makes strangers of family in the city? The pull that sends us outdoors whereas in the city, with everything from air conditioning to email to five hundred channels, it is always easier to stay in?

The beauty of sacrifice has largely been lost. What many cottagers want today is all the conveniences of the city—computers, television, cellphones, electric heat, easy access to shopping—at the same time as they enjoy all the delights of the cottage: the peace, the slow pace, the time for reflection. Perhaps they find time to read thick novels while they are downloading.

We are welcome to come here from the city, but if we bring too much of the city with us it will not be a matter of no longer being welcome, for we will find ourselves, unfortunately, among far too many of our own. It will, instead, be a far more serious matter of being too late.

The Flying Squirrel

Sometimes, magic happens. On an October weekend when, finally, nature decided to give a little back, some of us were sitting on the edge of a small, still lake waiting for the moon to rise when, suddenly, a winged beast flew by and landed, scrambling, on the trunk of a tall hemlock.

In my half-century of staring at everything that moves in the bush—from small toads to large bears—there remain a number of creatures that have never bothered to reveal themselves within eyesight. I have heard a lynx call, but never seen one. I have seen a wolverine along the side of a road, but never in the wild. And I have never seen the flying squirrel in full, glorious flight.

At first we thought it must have been a bat, but a bat smoothly gliding rather than flapping and twisting in the usual *Star Wars* fighter fashion. It came out of a stunningly clear night sky, swooped across the front of the porch, dipped, turned, and slammed in a flurry of scratch onto the hemlock, quickly scrambling up into the higher branches.

"Flying squirrel," someone said, and instantly everyone else knew that is exactly what it had been, though no one, oddly enough, had ever seen one outside of zoos and science centres, despite the fact the tiny squirrels with the elastic skin are said to be common in this part of the country.

Not a big thing, but these last few precious weekends are more about the little things, anyway. Like the unexpected break in the weather that produced one of the nicest days of the year. Like the ruffed grouse that seem to explode from each turn on the path, frightening the dogs that, somewhere in their confused lineage, were intended to be hunters. Like the family of merganser ducks still fishing in the shallows.

Mergansers are, surely, the most "socialist" of Canadian birds, with their summer-long daycare programs, their orderly processions about the shoreline, and their dedication to sharing. Now, however, it is clear the old order has broken down. There are only four ducklings now, the mother indistinguishable from her June hatchlings and the others lost to various predators. They follow nothing now but their own instincts, which will shortly take them away from these waters, perhaps never to return.

Here at the end of a dirt road that twists through a hardwood bush that is right now the colour of pumpkin and blood, it is time to haul in the dock, empty out the pantry, sock in enough dry wood for a few winter escapes, and, one day far too soon, go for the last long paddle of the year when it seems only moments ago we celebrated the first.

It has been a weekend when it has poured rain and sunshine in equal quantities, when fires have been all we talked about and when fires have barely been necessary, when those who are old enough to know better have insisted on one more swim—and will surely insist on one *final* swim come Thanksgiving weekend.

And a time, as well, when a small, furry creature never before seen has dropped in out of the hunter's moon. A small reminder that, no matter how perfectly, how completely, we think we know a place, we are continually surprised by the mysteries it contains.

October 11

12°C. Light breeze. The final day of the last holiday weekend before Christmas. It is supposed to be a celebration but no one is celebrating. We could say we're too busy, but that wouldn't be the real reason—the real reason is that we're in mourning. This is always the toughest day of the year. Water to shut off, draining to be done, antifreeze to put in, pipes to blow free, a refrigerator to empty and shut down, a pantry to check through, wood to cut, windows to seal, tears to shed.

Thanksgiving Unplugged

For a while, it looked as if the turkey might have to be cooked on a camp stove. It was a weekend in which the weather forecasters capped off a year equal to that enjoyed by the political pollsters—sunny and eighteen degrees called for, rainy and eight degrees calling in.

It was a weekend in which the leaves and wind peaked at the same time—the dirt road in like a drive through a spinning kaleidoscope—first the leaves coming down, then the trees. Or at least enough of them to take down power lines all across the Canadian Shield.

At times there were as many as fifteen gathered around the fireplace in this small cabin at the edge of the lake, far more than the fire marshal would ever allow if this part of the country had such a thing as roaming fire marshals.

And yet—given the unexpected power outage and the increasing possibility of naphtha-flavoured drumsticks— even that insufferably smug guy from the Canadian Tire ads would have been welcome to dinner, so long as he brought along his shiny new generator. For all we know, there might even be a special Canadian Tire attachment to carve the bird, and perhaps even one to do the dishes.

The winds may have been high and the batteries low, but still there were certain advantages to the situation. No electricity meant no communication, which meant no news from the outside, and not once did anyone ask if they might plug in a laptop and tie up the phone line while "I just quickly check my email." It has always been a world where cellphones cannot penetrate, but this weekend it became, however briefly, a world in which there was no connection at all.

Power outages are odd creatures in cottage country. They often become more about bragging than worrying. Old skills—pumping lamps, tying mantles, pouring camp gas, cooking over campfires, reading by coal oil lamp—are, at least in the beginning, a delight to discover. It is different, and so long as it is also harmless, it has its own pleasures.

There was a Christmas in the city many years back when these children who lounge about the floors playing guitars and singing were very much younger and the lights suddenly went off. One moment all was completely normal—television roaring, ghetto blasters pounding, Christmas lights blinding—and the next moment it was not normal at all. It was totally black. And completely silent.

The silence was the strangest part. No one said a word. Unlike at the cabin, there were no flashlights strategically placed within easy reach. There was, instead, the sound of soft scrambling as the small bodies of children and kittens and dogs found their way to the kitchen, and then the quick scrape of match over sandpaper as a very different kind of light was produced. Pale and yellow, it sent shadows leaping against the wall.

"Neat!" one of them shouted out as if some new present had just been unwrapped from under the tree.

We used the match to find the single flashlight, the flashlight to find the two ornamental coal oil lamps, and other matches to light the two lamps, the fireplace, and enough candles to turn the city house into a shadow-leaping home that felt warmer than perhaps it ever had. The children had never seen such magic.

"It's beautiful here," one of them said.

"It's like being at a cottage," another noticed.

And everyone agreed. It was not just the light, but the silence, as if for once in the city you might hear a squirrel scamper across the roof rather than the burst of a laugh track from the television room.

The children, so very small then, retrieved their comforters from their beds and came back to the fire, where they lay on the floor and wrapped themselves tight as tomorrow's butterflies while I fed the fire. They began talking, perhaps not surprisingly, about being at the lake.

"Remember the snapping turtle?" someone asked.

"Remember the deer antler by the sand pit?" another added.

I remember standing by the front window watching headlights sweep up and down the snowbanks and remembered not deer antlers but another house in the bush, where those same lamps just lighted would once cast enough light for an old ranger to work on his crossword puzzles while his wife fussed over the Christmas baking. It was the same silence, the same light, the same simple pleasure in small memories and small achievements.

"Remember the big toad?" the youngest asked.

But before anyone could recall it, the power surged back on. Lights. Television. Tapes. Buzzers. Clocks. But the most interesting new sound came from the children.

"Booooo!" one of them started.

"BOOOOOOO!" the others joined in.

It had been a false surge. The power failed again, the coal oil lamps, not even blown out, regained their place of glory. The children cheered. And the two of us, while the kids returned to their simple memories of the year just past, went about the house flicking off every imaginable electrical switch, making sure the power couldn't come snapping on again and break this remarkable spell.

Twenty years have now passed since that long-ago Christmas when the power in the city went off. Now, at the lake, with the power lines down, somewhere, these same children were grown adults, but still sitting on floors, wrapped in blankets, and close to the fire.

There was none of the regular music booming out, just that produced by a guitar, *acoustic,* voices that ranged from the angelic to desperately in need of duct tape, and memories that, for the most part, seemed incapable of moving beyond the first chorus.

Thanksgiving Weekend Unplugged. Such a curious creation, this Canadian Thanksgiving. This particular year it falls forty-five days before it arrives in the United States. Unlike the United States, no pilgrims ever landed in Canada. It is hard to imagine corn, let alone fat turkeys and cranberries, being shared by welcoming Native parties with the likes of Ericsson, Cabot, Cartier, Champlain, Hudson, Frobisher, Cook, Vancouver, et al. Perhaps moose nostrils. Or beaver paws. Or partridge stew and serviceberries.

The Canadian Thanksgiving celebrates harvest in a country where harvest as often means the sea in spring or the forest in winter and where, this very day, the fresh vegetables cooking on the stove probably came from California, or even South America, or were picked and frozen and shipped from another part of this country in, for all we know from the confusing jumble of this old freezer in the cabin, another century.

Sometimes it seems as if this is just another misplaced Canadian holiday, just as the true Canadian New Year is actually Labour Day, when everything begins again and all the important resolutions are made. *Thanksgiving,* for a good portion of this sprawling, northern country might be better held in mid-March, to salute survival. Or the May 24th weekend, when, instead of celebrating a dead Queen's birthday, we set off fireworks to welcome back the time of year that, in this part of the world, rules forever. And yet the "forever" that seems to stretch before you on May 24 soon winds down into a rather acute, and cursed, "now."

This is always the saddest time of all at a lake. The water is down, rendering the docks meaningless. The lake on a cold, rainy weekend like this is grey, gloomy, and threatening rather than sparkling blue and inviting—and yet there are several people here, from late teens to far too old to know better, who insist on going in swimming each Thanksgiving just to prove they are alive ... or is it *insane*?

There are walks for those who prefer windbreakers to swimsuits. And there is even one old dog who wasn't supposed to make Labour Day, let alone Thanksgiving, but who insists on hobbling along.

There is the final work to do. The canoe someone hauled down for a last morning paddle must now be hauled up for winter. There is water to shut off, pipes to drain, hoses to bleed. The wood box must be packed with both dry hardwood and thin, dry kindling—whatever it takes to get this place bearable a few minutes faster when we next come in winter.

Out at the country dump, the cars are lined up as if it, briefly, has become the border between one world and another, the summer waste being dropped off before the vehicles head off toward the paved roads, the city, and the looming concerns of winter radials, ice scrapers, and an ample supply of windshield fluid.

A deer, a small buck with new antlers, darts across the road near the dump, his own new coat now dark brown and thick enough to handle everything short of a logging truck bumper.

Surrounded by reality, we reluctantly begin to accept it.

The rain lets up, the wind dies down, the power comes on after a day and a night, the coal oil lamps are put away again—no "Boos" this time from the younger ones—and the threat of naphtha turkey is soon forgotten.

And then, just when least expected, magic strikes. Real power. Stunning power. Ultimate power. In the afternoon, just as the last of the boats still on the lake is hauled out at the government dock, the clouds suddenly break apart and the sun comes through for the first time since the forecasters promised it. The lake turns instantly blue, and calms. The few leaves still in the trees flash their colours and beckon walkers and old dogs and cameras.

And believe me, if it were at all possible to pull a switch somewhere and keep Thanksgiving Unplugged for a while longer, there is not a person here who would not try it. Whatever it takes to hang on to what matters most just a little while longer.

November 26

S M T W T F S
1 2 3 4 5 6
7 8 9 10 11 12 13
14 15 16 17 18 19 20
21 22 23 24 25 (26) 27
28 29 30

-4°C. This was supposed to be a last run to the cottage before the snow came. The water is off. The anti-freeze is in the pipes. The water line is out of the lake, the docks long since down, the boats long since up—but there's always one more thing. We are here to do a final check—put the outside chairs away, stock up and tarp the woodpiles for winter visits, make sure everything is locked up tight (more for mice than burglars). But, as sometimes happens, the snow beat us.

The Northern Lights

They were on this week. I have seen them before, but they are never the same. I have tried to describe them before, but they defy words even more than they challenge cameras and paintbrushes.

They are the Northern Lights, and to those who have stood and stared up in awe at their flickering and waving and dancing, and watched them shoot their white and green and red fingers from one side of the sky to the other, no other words are necessary. To those who have not seen them, may you one day be blessed by their presence.

They came this week on the heels of a solar eruption. While it may sound simpler to say they are merely reflections from high-suspended ice crystals, and while it is certainly more romantic to believe, as ancient Danes did, that they are caused by the flapping wings of vast numbers of swans headed north, they are actually just a phenomenon of physics: the sun sends out electrons that enter the upper atmosphere and interact with this planet's magnetic field.

But enough science. That's the "why," and pure chance seems to control the "when"—just as it does the other significant "w" in the equation of the Northern Lights: "where" you happen to be standing when they strike. Out of pure chance, I happened to be in the bush, where the sky still exists and has not been shelved by streetlights and city glow and the sheer necessity of never looking up when you had better be looking around. There was, on this perfect night, not a single other cabin on the lake with lights on, meaning two steps beyond the outhouse the sky turned into a home entertainment centre the size of the universe.

The bush of the Canadian Shield, however, has certain restrictions. The trees might be leafless but they are hardly branchless, and there are high spruce and hemlock spotted among the maple and birch. A better place to watch the show would be back of the government dock, where a small parking lot has been cleared. Better yet would be a farmer's field. Best of all, of course, would be anywhere in the great Canadian Prairie, where the sky is almost big enough to stage such a massive spectacle.

British anthologist Peter Haining has written that the Northern Lights are often taken as a portent of coming war. They were seen over London before war broke out in 1939 and flickered three successive nights over the heart of the United States just before the attack on Pearl Harbor in December of 1941. This belief is nothing new. In medieval times, Northern Lights were said to be a precursor of everything from coming war to plagues; some even thought they *caused* disasters.

But the messages have also been mixed. It has at times been thought they were messages from the Creator, to show He still cares, at other times that He is mightily displeased.

There is, according to a Norwegian website devoted to the lights, even an ancient belief that children must be herded inside and kept there while the sky is dancing, for fear the white shafts of light will suddenly sweep down and slice off their little heads. There being no children here at the moment and no belief that anyone, no matter how powerful, could control such an awe-inspiring show, we merely stood and watched, long into the night until the Northern Lights themselves seemed to grow weary and fade.

In the morning, there was snow on the ground. Not a sprinkling, but a substantial fall, enough to shovel if there was any sidewalk to shovel, which there is mercifully not. The snow covered the ground and the trees, covered the cabin and shed roofs, covered even the wood that still had to be split and stacked before the next visit—at which point you must shovel just to get in, let alone out.

But the lake has not frozen yet, and when the sun came out mid-morning it turned the water as blue as the sky had, at times, been bright white the night before. Around noon, there was a small "v" that could be seen cutting across the calm, blue water. It was thought, at first, to be a loon running late. Then a beaver. It turned out to be a deer, a doe swimming alone from the island to the cleared parking area.

There were hunters in the area, so perhaps she was looking for safer ground. But perhaps she was merely in search of better sight lines, should the miracle in the night sky return.

December 26

S	M	T	W	T	F	S
			1	2	3	4
5	6	7	8	9	10	11
12	13	14	15	16	17	18
19	20	21	22	23	24	25
(26)	27	28	29	30	31	

-22°C! This marks the third or fourth Boxing Day we have spent at the lake. The place is so full of visitors the dogs have to take turns lying down! But it's joyous and, we always say, the best place in the world to be on a day like this—once you get the heat cranked up.

Ice

There *are* whales down there!

Nearly five months had passed since that humiliating day in July when Denis, John, and I went out with my brand-new, sophisticated fish finder and discovered I somehow had neglected to turn it off "demonstration mode"—but suddenly it seemed there were indeed whales down there. And no beeping alarm or LCD readout required to indicate their presence.

We had come to the lake following a lovely Christmas spent in Ottawa. We drove over on Boxing Day under bright skies and caught and slipped and slid our way over a thin skin of snow that had fallen overnight along Limberlost Road. For a brief flight of fantasy, we thought we might be able to drive right in to the cabin. Heavy snow that had fallen in early December had melted away in the city, and though we had still lucked into a white Christmas, it was courtesy of a single fall that seemed more a coat of paint than a wall of its own.

For reasons that I have never understood, however, the weather at the cottage is rarely the weather described on the weather channel or picked up on the local radio station during the drive in. It is as if one heads up that last hill before the lake and slips into some new dimension that defies the meteorological charts. Winds rise where none have been promised, clouds appear where none were expected, and, more often than not, winter lies deeper and colder than anyone ever expected.

The last hill is never plowed by the district, though someone with a four-wheel drive had obviously taken a run at it a day or so earlier. If it wasn't impassable then, it certainly was now—deeply rutted all the way up to where he had come to his senses and, poorly, backed down again.

We parked at the usual spot near the gravel pit, slipped on heavier boots, loaded the groceries, air mattresses, sleeping bags, drinks, water, and extra shovels onto two toboggans and prepared, once again, to hike in to a cabin that was guaranteed to be much colder indoors than out.

It had been a funny winter, the snow coming, then vanishing, the ice barely formed on many of the lakes along Highway 60 and through Algonquin Park. There were fish shacks near the shore of Golden Lake, but open water yawning beyond; the Opeongo and Madawaska rivers still ran open and free, the quick water looking too cold to freeze solid. There was no packed snowmobile path to follow in as there usually is. But then again, the snow wasn't so deep you had to wade through it, as is often the case at this time of year.

We made it in almost effortlessly and, shortly, the fire was on and the cabin began filling up with people. All four of our kids had come along—a rarity in recent years, but they had insisted they all come together this year. Their cousins were also coming down from North Bay, bringing one friend. As well, two of Gordon's friends were on their way.

The cabin measures eight hundred square feet. It is forty feet long and twenty feet wide. We slept thirteen adults, two large dogs, and one dog the size of a fat mouse that night. That works out to fifty square feet per visiting creature—we refuse to count those creatures already there—and given the space required for refrigerator and stove, sink and unusable bathroom, tables, chairs, bookcases, backpacks, CD player, guitars, and, of course, fireplace and woodbin, it worked out to approximately six square inches per person a night—a wonder that we did not have to sleep, like horses, standing up.

And yet it was magnificent, even for those who found themselves picking their way, like someone crossing a shallow creek, through the bodies late at night for a desperate run to the outhouse.

After the materialistic flurry of Christmas, it was cathartic to once again haul out the board games, the cards. After the traffic of holiday malls, it was a delight to work with only two paths: one heading up to the outhouse, one heading down to the lake, with no room to pass on either. And after too much turkey and drink, it was glorious to get out and walk, either up through the woods with snowshoes, or out along the ice—now eight inches thick, the auger told us—and around the lake for as long as anyone wished to wander under a pale blue sky, a weak winter sun, and, mercifully, precious little wind.

We were the only ones on the entire lake. And in the afternoon, when the sun rose as high in the southern sky as it could get before dropping like a slammed basketball around four o'clock, it was almost *warm* in those rare pockets along the shore where the cedars kept out the wind and the rocks caught and held what few rays were making it so far north.

The lake was, in those precious moments, what American writer Edward Abbey said of the Utah national park where he once worked, "the most beautiful place on earth." "There are many such places," the author of *Desert Solitaire* wrote. "Every man, every woman, carries in heart and mind the image of the ideal place, the right place, the one true home, known or unknown, actual or visionary."

And this was ours, *the right place, the one true home, known* ...

We walked from our bay around to the islands and down through the west bay toward the dam, our footprints following a trail laid out by two white-tailed deer as they had meandered along the shoreline nibbling at overhanging cedar branches.

"What's that sound?" one of the kids asked.

We all stopped, waiting. It was a sound absolutely strange, oddly familiar. It felt at times like the growl of a giant's stomach, at times like the wail of an animal in mourning. It sometimes sounded like a siren, warning; sometimes like a low, gentle moan, comforting. It sounded like whales calling.

"It's the ice forming," I said. "It's shifting and it's moving air pockets around. That's how you get those sounds."

"Weird," said someone.

"It's beautiful," said someone else.

And powerful, the ice also periodically cracking as old plates gave way to new ones, the lake like a newly forming world in constant flux—but you had to listen for it. It was another reminder—like the wind that felled the hemlock, the lovely pink lady's slipper, the awe of a summer lightning storm—that everything else is temporary: the docks, the buildings, even the people.

We stood by a point with a small campsite on it and simply listened to this little-known song of winter, the sounds at times coming at once, almost in harmony, at other times seeming to argue with each other as to which sound had dominance.

Never, not even on a wind-whipped day when the whitecaps threaten, have I ever felt the lake so alive. And yet, to the eye, not a single thing was happening. It was all in the ear. And in the imagination. Where all the best memories are kept.

January 1

S	M	T	W	T	F	S
						①
2	3	4	5	6	7	8
9	10	11	12	13	14	15
16	17	18	19	20	21	22
23	24	25	26	27	28	29
30	31					

-6°C. Bright and sunny. Snow-covered roads coming through Algonquin Park. Very little traffic. One moose. One fox. Dozens of ravens. No cars at all at the gravel pit. Long haul in by toboggan and snowshoe—but worth every bit of it.

Winter Cottaging

There was an item in the paper this week in which a Toronto television station claimed to have picked up a substantial market share of the Christmas Day viewing audience by showing four straight hours of nothing but a flaming fireplace.

Let me out of here!

It seemed like a good idea at the time, but for every hour the drive took to get back to the frozen lake less than a week after we'd been there, the snow seemed to rise a foot. No snow in the city, but it seemed a blizzard had struck cottage country. By the time we got here it was dark and the snow approximately the level of your bare butt if you didn't happen to be wearing underwear and snowshoes.

Fortunately, we had both on, as well as ski jackets and tuques and thick gloves and double-paired pants and thick, grey work socks, and a toboggan to carry the necessities in through the dark. Except, it is never quite so dark as imagined in the winter bush. Evening here is, in fact, more like a second daylight, but filtered, and with more shadows. It is a sensation denied the 80 percent of Canadians who live in urban centres where—paradoxically—excessive lighting makes nighttime seem too dark.

Even so, there is nothing quite so sweet as seeing a thin, yellow light flooding through the trees in the distance, the signal that cousins coming from the other direction have already reached the little cabin in the woods. There is smoke rising from the chimney, meaning the fire is on. With luck, the woodpile—perhaps even the outhouse—will have been dug out again, and perhaps someone has even been down to the lake and drilled a fresh hole into the ice for drinking water.

If there is scientific proof for the winter cottager's observation that "it's colder inside than out" on first arrival, I have not seen it. But I do believe it. We have often "warmed up" the place by firing up the woodburner and flinging open the doors and windows. When the children were smaller, they were sent out to play until their shivering question as to whether it was "okay to come inside yet?" could be answered by a nod. To arrive at a pre-heated cabin in the dead of winter is, perhaps, the greatest luxury available to Canadians.

It is so different here in winter. There is no one on the lake. If there were, they might also be in the lake, for the ice is still not all that safe. It formed, then there was a thaw, and now it is too uncertain. It is only as thick as a pane of glass beyond where the neighbour's diving dock has been anchored twice for the winter—once to the cement block that keeps it in the bay all summer, once to the ice that locks it all winter.

The thin ice has meant no snowmobiles howling up and down the lake as is normally the case at this time of year, and while some would count that a blessing, those who had to bring the supplies in by toboggan might argue they could have used the rolling, tightly packed trails the machines create with all their traffic coming to and from the lake.

This absence of machinery has re-created winter as history must have recorded the Canadian winter: the snow deep and impossibly white, the sound muffled by thick snow in the pines so that the noise of the city has receded far back in memory, never, with luck, to be found again.

One of the great curiosities of winter is that the days are actually longer—out of sheer busy-ness, from putting on more clothes to shovelling first, walking second—even though the light is decidedly weaker. But since we put so much more in, we should try to take more out.

Canadians, in fact, sometimes seem almost embarrassed by their long winter. At one point in the late 19th century, the federal government even banned the word "cold" from government brochures, insisting instead that the proper term was "buoyant." ("Christ—is it ever buoyant out!" doesn't sound right, does it?) Mercifully, most of us no longer pretend winter in Canada is anything but what it is—even with global warming.

Some will say that the catty British writer Frances Brooke was right a couple of hundred years back when she said, "Genius will never mount high, where the faculties of the mind are benumbed half the year." Well, call me dumb if you wish, but I happen to think there's something oddly comforting about a cold, cold winter where the snow runs so deep only toboggans and snowshoes can penetrate—especially given the state of today's world.

The advantages of winter cottaging—extreme cottaging, if you will—might be slight enough. You can, for example, actually see the moose in a photograph taken of one in winter. But there are real joys to be found in doing what at first seems much easier not to do at all.

I see I am not alone if I check the familiar log book on top of the fridge. There is even one entry where, after a week in March of fog and rain and a broken ice auger, someone has scribbled "No one wants to leave!" at the bottom of the final entry for that visit. An even earlier visit contains an entry by the eldest of the four, when she was then only nine: "I like it here even better than in the summer."

A moot point, at best, but there are some distinct advantages to a place where the only threat is nature itself and a truce can be easily reached by those with proper clothing, some rudimentary shelter and supplies, an axe, and a few matches.

Out here, the only leadership race is between the visiting dogs trying to see which can be first down the trail. And out here, the gold medal goes to those who come second and third—well after some other sucker has broken a trail up the hill to the outhouse. And perhaps even warmed up the seat.

Subnivian

I count any day good in which I learn a new word.

Subnivian.

I learned of the existence of this lovely word while standing, hip deep in snow, on the top of a rustic cabin deep in
the woods, though I could have used it several hours earlier
as I happened to be sitting—more accurately, hovering—in
the old outhouse back of the cabin and noticed that something had chewed through the particleboard at a level
considerably below the outside snow line.

Beyond this new entrance to the outhouse there
appeared to be a shallow air pocket between the snow and
the ground, a maze of runways and getaways for whatever
small creature it was that believed it could survive a cold
winter in this rundown outhouse. A cold winter, perhaps;
a warm summer, never.

We had come to the lake on account of a warning in the
local weekly that snow build-up on area roofs was
approaching the danger level and another on the Weather
Network that a nasty storm would soon be sweeping in,
with everything possible from freezing rain to a thousand
metres of snow.

Perhaps a year ago I might have ignored such warnings. But one spring we found the neighbouring cabin flattened when we made our first foray north. The culprit then was wind and trees, not snowfall, but still nature, and subject to all the wild mood swings that make up this unstable country: sunny in Vancouver; sleet shifting to fog in Newfoundland; 60 percent chance of catastrophe at the edge of Algonquin Park.

We trekked in from where the plows turn back. The four of us—including two daughters, the other two siblings claiming prior commitments—hauled in dry clothes and extra mittens and additional shovels by toboggan and snowshoe. It was, as the children like to tell their friends, uphill both directions, with wolves hanging from our throats and nothing but a single, worn stone to make soup for the weekend—but we persevered, and eventually we found the cabin still standing, albeit creaking and shaking under 40,000 tonnes of snow.

We know much of our time will be spent shovelling during winter visits because we get in so rarely during the off-season. The rest of the time, those reading this in prison libraries might like to know, we have helicopter surveillance, free-roaming Dobermans, and trip wires strategically placed through the woods so any potential break-and-enter artist will instantly be hoisted to the highest branches by his ankle and left to the mercy of the elements.

Not far from this spot, two legendary brothers made their winter living for years by offering a set fee to keep an eye on roofs once cottagers headed back to their lives in faraway cities, mostly American. The brothers, of course, never lifted a finger all winter. The summer visitors would return to find their retreat still standing—and happily offer a bonus. In the only known instance of a roof caving in, the brothers shook their heads sadly and said a terrible storm had come up in late winter, and while they had gallantly struggled to reach their charges in time, they had unfortunately come up one short.

I admire excellent excuses. And it being well established that only men suffer heart attacks while shovelling snow (even if this is an urban myth, it's a handy one), I was determined to do as little as possible, and so I happened to tell the story of the new hole in the outhouse and the little world beyond. That, one of the daughters said, would be "subnivian."

This happens quite often as children grow older around you. There is a time when the parent is the font of all knowledge. Then comes a time, usually around grade six, when homework moves beyond the parent. Eventually comes higher education, at which point the sole purpose of the parent is to send money and stay out of the way.

Her lecture, however, was entrancing. There is, I now know, a thin little world that exists only in winter, a pocket that often forms between the ground and deep snow where creatures of a certain size are able to live relatively comfortably and largely protected, oblivious for months to the outside world.

The other daughter suggested that the snow was so high on the roof that we could build our own network of tunnels and live in our own subnivian world. I found that oddly attractive, given the endless bad news scrolling on CNN this particular winter.

And, in a way, we did live that life for three days and two nights. We shovelled and slept, and, of course, took turns sucking on the stone for nourishment. No newspapers, no internet, no telephone, no visitors. Not once in three days was the radio even turned on.

We left with the snow piled so high around the cabin you could see neither in nor out. The two girls who did most of the shovelling finished off by somersaulting off the roof and we headed back out the same way we had come in, uphill, with wolves tearing at our throats and clouds moving in from the east. And then, as sometimes happens in this country, it began to snow.

March 19

S	M	T	W	T	F	S
		1	2	3	4	5
6	7	8	9	10	11	12
13	14	15	16	17	18	⑲
20	21	22	23	24	25	26
27	28	29	30	31		

-7°C. A frightening drive over—whiteouts so thick as we neared Algonquin Park it seemed, at times, as if we were floating in one of those little plastic globes you shake and turn upside down. We stopped a while at the East Gate parking lot, decided to turn back, and then decided, on the spur of the moment, to follow a logging truck through— even if it meant chasing his rear lights right off the Smoke Lake lookout! But we're here, we're happy, and not once since we arrived have I been asked to hand over a credit card—so what could be better?

March Break

It was a time when the children were much younger and the annual March Break from school was about to begin. I had been peeking through the office blinds at the unshovelled driveway and the unplowed street. Where there was supposed to be clean, white beach sand, there was only dirty, white snow. Where there should have been palm trees waving, there was only a rusted-out Christmas tree that should have gone weeks earlier.

Way back on New Year's Day, it had been dragged out to the end of the driveway for pickup, but a freak rain and sudden freeze had locked it solid into the snow bank. I couldn't free it with a military flamethrower, let alone the axe. The garbage collectors had yanked at it the first few times they passed by but gave up sometime in late February. So there the sad Christmas tree sat, growing ever more brown and spindly, while we could only dream of going darker ourselves and shaking out our own branches.

Like most Canadians, we had found increasingly over the years that we were never where we expected to be come the March Break. Twenty years earlier, the plan had been simple and straightforward: *this* would be the year we joined the rest of the country on a Caribbean island. We would even set up a separate account, put a little aside each month, pay now and fly later. The vacation of a lifetime. Only someone forgot to open an account. And someone else forgot to put a little aside.

A decade earlier, the Caribbean plan had changed: we would, instead, join the rest of Canada in Florida. We would fly down. Then we would *drive* down. But again, someone forgot to put enough aside.

Soon enough, the plan changed yet again; we would go to … Vermont. We would learn to ski. We would dress sharply. We would have a chalet, a sheepskin rug, a crackling fire, Chinese take-out for six. Naturally, someone forgot to save up enough money to pay even for the take-out.

As those annual March Breaks crept ever closer, panic would begin to set in. Sobbing children would burst in the back door with yet another tale of a classmate—whose parents, I suspected, were either part of the Colombian drug cartels or else had taken the money the rest of us put into high-tech and stashed it under the mattress—about to head off for Acapulco … Orlando … the Bahamas … Venezuela … Bermuda … the seventh ring of Saturn.

That was around the time when we finally admitted something had to be done. Something, mind you, that could be done with no money, no new clothes, no eight-hundred-kilometre-a-day turnpike marathons, no motels, no fast food, and no souvenir sweatshirts—but something that was ... well ... different.

That's where the cabin in the snowy woods comes in. But the first time out it took some imaginative selling points. The same mouth that only short years ago was talking about mile-long runs at Jay Peak would now have to pitch, with a straight face, the breathtaking thrills of snowshoeing—with no chairlifts to haul you up the hills.

The same mouth that once talked of Caribbean water so clear that a snorkler can see forever would now have to argue that the absolute definition of pure delight is an axe and a pail and nothing but two feet of ice between you and enough crystal-clear water to carry back up to do the dishes.

The same mouth that had then talked about Disney World and the Magic Kingdom would now have to sell new rides, like the Outhouse Lift, in which the naked body must somehow remain suspended in mid-air over a 40-below circle of wood for as long as it takes.

Some outhouse users never look down. But we have never looked back.

The World's Largest Rink

If you think voices carry across water in summer, keep your mouth shut in winter. Gord and I are standing in the middle of the bay and we are singing the national anthem. Being good—no, *excellent*—Canadians, of course, we have no idea what the words are to "O Canada" beyond the first verse and soon switch to the other national anthem, the one we all know by heart: Stompin' Tom Connors's "The Hockey Song." Neither of us can sing very well, but we both skate fine—and once a year we try to take to the lake in a fashion that is quite beyond the realm of possibility in summer.

We used to come out during March Break and now arrive during Reading Week, though I cannot ever recall seeing anyone under thirty with a book in hand at this late-winter time of year.

We come out and shovel off a rink, when necessary, and play a hockey game. No lockout, no admission, no fans, no score apart from the ones we argue over. Once in a while, on a rare late winter's day, there is no need to shovel, for the lake will have been swept as clean and shiny by wind and early thaw and late freeze as if a giant Zamboni had made the rounds as we slept. There is, truly, nothing in summer to compare to it.

If my son thinks he can do certain things on a wake-board, I can do more on this same body of water wearing sharp steel blades, with nothing but my own legs to provide the necessary thrusts and turns. *360s?* Ha! Just watch me spin out on that sharp corner by the big island. *Flips?* Hey! Where did that snowdrift come from?

If there are shoals in summer, there are ice-fishing holes in winter. If there are waves in summer, there are snow-mobile tracks in winter. If there are cold spots all over the lake in summer, there is, alas, only one in winter. Right by the fireplace.

The rules of summer cottaging are as complicated as the parliamentary rules of order, but the rules of winter cottaging are so simple they barely pad out this paragraph: don't go in until the temperature inside passes the temperature outside; keep a Styrofoam circle around for the outhouse; don't melt down the snow from anywhere near where the dog has travelled.

It is a time so quiet, so special, so different that it has always astonished me how few cottagers make the effort to go in. I would guess the vast majority on this isolated lake have never even seen their place in winter. They can relax—we look for them. In the windows ... under the decks ... even, on a rare occasion, behind an unlocked door. We see not only what might have been done last summer, but what needs to be done this coming summer. A new deck railing across the lake. A new dock crib at the landing ... And, of course, it gets us thinking about what truly matters: things we have to do ourselves once we can get at them.

These are the days when we wake to surprise thaws, when we smell pine needles where a small patch has melted along the north side of the bay, when we hear the ice groan and sometimes give and know that it is only a matter of days—okay, weeks—until the ice goes out and we come back in.

Back to a time when the true anthem of the country is heard in the high pines. And everyone knows the music by heart.

March 29

S	M	T	W	T	F	S
		1	2	3	4	5
6	7	8	9	10	11	12
13	14	15	16	17	18	19
20	21	22	23	24	25	26
27	28	(29)	30	31		

5°C. Bright and beautiful. There are two lakes out there, the old lake under the ice, and the new, melted lake over the ice. Winter is finally giving in a little. The snowmobile tracks rise out of the new lake like stumpy railway trestles and it's worrisome to see one roar past, slush flying from the skis. The ice should be entirely out of the bay within a couple of weeks—early this year.

The Cottage
of the Mind

It certainly does get around. In the past two years alone it's been to every province, a large number of the States, and twice to Europe. Quite a cottage, isn't it? I'm always amazed at how they try and sell these things in the local paper: "Northern exposure, 160 feet of shoreline, no winter access." Words that come about as close to a useful description as "Male wearing balaclava."

What I'm talking about is a cottage with 24,000 *miles* of shoreline—with year-round access from anywhere in the world. That's mine. Perhaps yours, as well. Mine can be found summers on a small, cold, and clear lake off Highways 35 and 60, where an osprey nests in the high rocks. But it can also be found the rest of the year on Air Canada flights where the guy in the next seat is pouring back too many drinks and wanting to talk politics, in distant hotel rooms where the only choice on television is between *American Idol* and *Canadian Idol*, or in an office where the urgent morning email concerns a Mazda in the parking lot with its lights left on.

"I wouldn't have a cottage," people keep telling us. "You only get to use it for two or three weeks of the year. What's the point?" *The point?* Usually, we say nothing—for how do you explain, without causing a confidential report to end up in Human Resources, that those of us who do have cottages use them *every single day of the year?*

Mine is on my computer, a screen saver that I can change as the mood fits: the view from the deck, a long shot down the lake, a sweeping twilight photograph of the small bay we are on. My cottage is there, and it is also in my imagination whenever required. I think about it while shovelling the driveway. I visit it when I'm stuck in traffic.

I worry about it, not deep-vein thrombosis, when flying across multiple time zones. That is not me snoring on the couch in mid-afternoon; it is me planning and organizing, doing the grunt work required for another perfect summer at the lake. For those of us who know that a place at the lake is a year-round retreat—even if the township won't plow all the way in—the cottage is C.S. Lewis's wardrobe, Alice's mirror, Track 9 ¾ for Harry Potter's Hogwarts Express.

It is what we use to get away, even when physically we cannot get away. It is where we go to escape, to dream, to plan, even to visit, thinking fondly of friends on the lake we have not seen since the previous summer, thinking of favourite places where we like to paddle shortly after dawn, the lake still steaming with the mysteries of the night. It is, as well, what we hold onto, our Linus's blanket, when things don't go quite as planned or hoped.

Those of us who hold cottages and cabins and even special campsites dear to the heart find this a difficult matter to explain adequately to others. If some wish to call it denial, we cannot argue, for the idea of summer escape is what makes January, February, and March possible. It is what makes a summer workday bearable, with or without air conditioning. Because we know the weekend is coming and we are going.

Warm Spots

Curious how we shout out to the world when we come across a "warm spot" while swimming, yet keep such discoveries to ourselves while walking. We encounter them regularly at this time of year, and they strike like life itself among those of us who can hardly wait for the snow to melt and the ice to go and the season that matters most to return once again.

Henry James once said that the two most beautiful words in the English language must be "summer afternoon," and there is not one among us, at the moment, who would disagree.

I usually find my walking "warm spots" in Alice Wilson Woods, a small park near our Ottawa-area home where I take the dog every day at noon, where neither rain nor snow nor sleet nor hail can keep us from our appointed rounds. We take pride in going in tough weather, but, quite frankly, we are both sorely tired of winter by now. Both of us treasure those moments when, in a sudden turn along the trail, the March sun will suddenly wash over us with a new awareness. When the wind moves through the high pines these days, you can almost swear it sighs in relief.

It is moments like this when I am reminded, once again, how often Canada seems not to go by the calendars of the rest of the world. Labour Day, we have all agreed, is really the start of the New Year in this country. And while February 2 may be Groundhog Day in the U.S., it may as well be called Polar Bear Day in Canada. The year here does not quarter, as it does in so much of the rest of the world, but splits virtually in two, winter and summer, with spring and fall but fragments of each. We jump the gun on summer; we wish we held a weapon that could hold up winter.

I have timed spring at Alice Wilson Woods in the city and at our little cabin at the lake and they run along the same lines. The snow melts, the grass comes up, the wildflowers sprout—and *summer* is declared. Some years, spring lasts a few weeks, but one year we had it down to approximately an hour and a half. I went for a nap at the end of winter; I woke at the beginning of summer.

I mark the precise return to delight with the first open trillium. Forty-some years ago, my sister Ann, then a teenager, headed off into the spring woods near our home in Huntsville with a pail and a shovel and returned with a bucketful of trilliums. She then carefully transplanted them under a large maple while her three brothers warned that the police were on their way to arrest her on some arcane, or imagined, provincial law that said the picking of wild trilliums was worse than parking in front of a fire hydrant.

The police never came to take her away, however, and the trilliums took magnificently. Today, though Ann was lost far too young to cancer, the maple has long since been felled for safety reasons, and someone else now lives in the old house on Reservoir Hill, Ann's wildflower legacy comes up each year, white as fresh-fallen snow yet filled with incredible warmth.

You have to be alert to catch spring in Canada. We treat it more like a door we have to get through than a room we linger in—perhaps because it is so much less than a real season and fluctuates so between winter's hangover and summer's tease.

"Spring is distrusted here," Alden Nowlan once wrote of his New Brunswick home, "for it deceives — / snow melts upon the lawns, / uncovering / last fall's dead leaves." And yet we can hardly wait to sweep away last fall's dead leaves and find, once again, the country we love best, no matter what the condition. We search the skies for returning geese, the backyard for robins, the garden for crocuses, and the basement for light jackets.

We push up summer at the cabin, as well, heading up as soon as it is possible to drive in the road the township refuses to plow and hauling the barbecue out of the outhouse the moment we arrive. The cabin door pops open like a wine cork, releasing a musty, familiar smell that is oddly warming despite the interior always being colder than the outside.

Some of the cottage journal entries over the years seem to defy logic: *"The weather is very warm—summery—but the water is still extremely cold,"* says a May 8 entry from several years ago. *"There is ice on the lake and snow in the bushes. The kids went swimming."*

Don't worry—they soon found a warm spot. Right next to the fireplace. Where they stood, shivering. In part from winter's last blast. In larger part from the first hint of the beloved summer to come.

April 16

17° C. Warm and sunny, the air perfectly still. The sun feels so good on bare arms. The windows are down for what seems the first time since September. And while there is still snow in the bush, there are no bugs yet. No one has called to say otherwise, so we will presume the ice is still in. Perhaps we will get there in time to see it go out. There's just enough light that, if we decide on a whim to head out at noon, we should still get there before dark. Two weeks into Daylight Saving and we are already spending everything we can get our hands on.

Acknowledgments

The bulk of these tales appeared in somewhat modified form in *Cottage Life* magazine. The remainder, not many, appeared at various times in *The Globe and Mail, National Post,* and *Ottawa Citizen.* All were abridged for this publication, some changed very lightly, a few entirely rewritten, and a number of pieces are original works.

The author owes his longtime editor at Penguin Canada, Barbara Berson, for finding a format that brought everything together. He is also grateful to managing editor Tracy Bordian for pulling it off, to Soapbox for their remarkable design work, and to artist Jason Schneider for giving the book a voice beyond words. Two editing friends, Alex Schultz and Edie Van Alstine, offered terrific suggestions, including, I must admit, the scrapping of certain work to which I was inexplicably attached. Thanks as well to Bruce Westwood, Natasha Daneman, and Amy Tompkins at Westwood Creative Artists for seeing a book in all these years of cottage writing and for staying on my case until it was done.

Above all, however, I owe the family—Ellen, Kerry, Christine, Jocelyn, and Gordon—for letting me tell their various adventures at the lake. And we all owe a very special dog, Bandit, who spent fifteen years herding us back to shore and who left us better people than when she adopted us for her own.